SMALL GROUP
OUTREACH

SMALL GROUP
OUTREACH

How to Begin and Lead Outreach
Bible Study Groups

Kurt W. Johnson

REVIEW AND HERALD® PUBLISHING ASSOCIATION
HAGERSTOWN, MD 21740

This book was
Edited by Jack Calkins
Designed by Helcio Deslandes
Cover Photos © Review and Herald
Typeset: 10/11 Korinna

PRINTED IN U.S.A.

96 95 94 93 92   10 9 8 7 6 5 4 3 2

Library of Congress Cataloging-in-Publication Data
Johnson, Kurt W., 1950-
    Small group outreach: how to begin and lead outreach Bible study groups / Kurt W. Johnson.
        p.   cm.
    Includes bibliographical references.
    1. Seventh-day Adventists—Membership. 2. Adventists—Membership.
3. Sabbatarians—Membership. 4. Church group work.
5. Small groups. 6. Bible—Study. 7. Evangelistic work. I. Title.
BX6154.J63   1991
253'.7—dc20
                                                                    90-25165
                                                                        CIP

ISBN 0-8280-0616-4

Contents

Preface

Welcome to a new and exciting adventure in personal Bible study for yourself, and an effective method of outreach to your neighbors! I am positive that you will find the concept of Home Bible Study groups a refreshing approach to sharing the good news about Jesus with those living near you. The approach is nonoffensive and is not a threat to an individual's current religious status. It is an approach that permits you to establish a friendship and dialogue based on biblical truths. It prepares the way for an in-depth look at Seventh-day Adventists' understanding of Scripture.

The concept developed in this book grew out of a need that was expressed by various church members and pastors in the Oregon Conference of Seventh-day Adventists.

After nearly 1,000 members and pastors joined forces to present Bible teaching seminars in homes, churches, and public buildings, two observations were expressed: First, that seminars held in homes were more relaxed and personal, allowing for relationships to be formed very quickly. This provided for an open atmosphere in which fewer non-SDA individuals dropped out. The close relationships gave them the support to continue attending when difficult doctrinal issues were discussed. Second, the individuals attending had varying backgrounds with the Bible and SDA doctrines. Many times class members would drop out because a teaching was presented that they were personally unprepared to deal with. The thought was expressed that we needed sets of lessons dealing with basic issues from books of Scripture that would prepare people for deeper doctrinal Bible study at a later time. It's simply more fruitful when we provide a slow, steady, ongoing learning experience, maintaining the students' by developing true friendships. Thus, the Home Bible Study group concept was developed.

After careful analysis and prayer, a team strategy was organized under the leadership of Don Jacobsen, president of the Oregon Conference of Seventh-day Adventists.

Garrie Williams, ministerial director in the Oregon Conference, wrote the first study guides and directed the program. Larry Evans, special assistant to the president of the Oregon Conference, developed leaders' guides to be used with Elder Williams' lessons.

Kurt Johnson, personal ministries director in Oregon, organized and directed the training of the church members to conduct the home small group meetings. To assist in the training process, instruction manuals were developed by Kurt Johnson. This book follows several years of personal training experience, learning from experienced group leaders, personal experience in leading small groups, and four revisions of training manuals.

As you read this book, please remember that it has been written with the sincere desire, hope, and prayer that it will be a useful tool in learning one method in sharing with your neighbors the benefits of the abundant life in Jesus Christ revealed in the books of the Bible.

1

Spiritual Essentials

I was 4 years old and alone in the living room. My little mind was awhirl, wondering what to do next. Cautiously I made my way to the forbidden zone—the area near the floor heater on the far side of the room.

Examining the large electrical outlet, I was intrigued by the slots that went in various directions. With insatiable curiosity I scrutinized the 220-volt receptacle and spied a hairpin lying on the floor. Picking it up, I began probing the slots. Immediately a loud bang resounded as a ball of flame jumped out at me. I was knocked to the floor!

As I lay dazed and wondering what had occurred, my mother rushed to my rescue. Through that event a lesson of power was indelibly written upon my mind.

Upon reflection, I am reminded of the apostle's experience recorded in Acts 2:1-4,14-21: "When the day of Pentecost came, they were all together in one place. Suddenly a sound like the blowing of a violent wind came from heaven and filled the whole house where they were sitting. They saw what seemed to be tongues of fire that separated and came to rest on each of them. All of them were filled with the Holy Spirit and began to speak in other tongues as the Spirit enabled them." "Then Peter stood up with the Eleven, raised his voice and addressed the crowd: 'Fellow Jews and all of you who are in Jerusalem, let me explain this to you; listen carefully to what I say. These men are not drunk, as you suppose. It's only nine in the morning! No, this is what was spoken by the prophet Joel: "In the last days, God says, I will pour out my Spirit on all people. Your sons and daughters will prophesy, your young men will see visions, your old men will dream dreams. Even on my servants, both men and women, I will pour out my Spirit in those days, and they will prophesy. I will show wonders in the heaven above and signs on the earth below, blood and fire and billows of smoke. The sun will be turned to darkness and the moon to blood before the coming of the great and glorious day of the Lord. And everyone who calls on the name of the Lord will be saved" ' "(NIV).

Ellen White, in reflecting upon this promise and experience, made the following comment in the *Review and Herald* of August 25, 1896: "We should pray as earnestly for the descent of the Holy Spirit as the disciples prayed on the Day of Pentecost. If they needed Him at that time, we need Him more today. All manner of false doctrines, heresies, and deceptions are misleading the minds of men; and without the Spirit's aid, our efforts to present divine truth will be in vain. We are living in the time of the Holy Spirit's power. He is seeking to diffuse Himself through the agency of humanity, thus increasing His influence in the world. For if any man drinks of the water of life, it will be in him a well of water springing up into everlasting life; and the blessing will not be confined to himself, but will be shared by others."

Jesus promised power to every believer. In John 14:15-26 we read: "If you love me, you will obey what I command. And I will ask the Father, and he will give you another Counselor to be with you forever—the Spirit of truth. The world cannot accept him, because it neither sees him nor knows him. But you know him, for he lives with you and will be in you. I will not leave you as orphans; I will come to you. . . . All this I have spoken while still with you. But the Counselor, the Holy Spirit, whom the Father will send in my name, will teach you all things and will remind you of everything I have said to you" (NIV).

Yes, God desires each of us to be Spirit-empowered men and women! Pray for the Spirit, desire to be filled by the Spirit, claim the promise of the infilling of the Spirit, and you will receive POWER! God has promised—and His Word is sure!

As you become involved in small group ministry, remember that your ability to minister is based upon your own spiritual well-being. Your own private time for Bible study and prayer is essential to your group. As you begin to plan and work toward your small group meeting, consider doing the following:

A. Set aside one hour each day for God.
B. Spend part of the hour praying for:
   1. Your own relationship with God.
   2. A good response from the community.
   3. Support from the local church.
   4. Your teaching abilities to be Spirit-filled.
   5. Decisions for Christ and baptisms.
   6. Outpouring of the Holy Spirit in latter rain proportions.
C. Bible study:
   1. Spend time restudying the book of the Bible your Home Bible Study guides cover.
   2. Find and write on cards God's promises of strength, faith, power, and soul winning.
D. Spirit of Prophecy
   1. Read Ellen White's comments on the subject matter and book of the Bible your study guide covers.
   2. Read Ellen White's comments on soul winning. *Gospel Workers* and *Evangelism* would be a good beginning point.
E. Meditation and Memorization:
   1. Memorize some of the promises you discovered in C. 2 above. Learn one each week.

Yes, small groups are a key ingredient of the local church. But as we consider small group ministry we must not overlook the power behind the small group principle. That power is the Holy Spirit.

CHAPTER

2

Small Groups in Early Church History

The book of Acts records the Holy Spirit's work in the fledgling church. Following Pentecost, dramatic growth resulted, not from any human power, but through the indwelling of the Holy Spirit in the disciples. Three thousand believers were added in 24 hours (Acts 4:1).

The preaching of the disciples in Jerusalem was so effective that the Jewish authorities banned them from the Temple, imprisoned Peter, and inflicted severe persecution (Acts 4, 5). The stringent acts of the Jewish leaders made it nearly impossible for the disciples to preach in Jerusalem. Consequently, the disciples left Jerusalem to preach in other parts of the continent. Luke states: "Those who were scattered went everywhere preaching the word" (Acts 8:4, NKJV).

As the disciples scattered throughout Judea and beyond, they stopped in various city synagogues and taught (Acts 26:19, 20). Paul, an educated scholar, found himself right at home teaching about Jesus to the Jewish community. However, resistance persisted, so the disciples turned repeatedly to the non-Jewish world.

The disciples' outreach involved more than public preaching. It also involved teaching and preaching in the homes of believers. Acts 20:20 reveals that Paul's methods included teaching "house to house." In his letter to the church at Colossae, Paul writes about the church at Laodicea, which met in the home of Nymphas (Col. 4:15). Other New Testament references to home meetings are 1 Corinthians 16:19

13

and Romans 16:3-5 which mention meetings in the home of Priscilla and Aquila and Acts 16:40 which mentions Lydia's home.

One reason the church met in homes was because they were banned from public meetings in the Jewish synagogues. Consequently, homes became the foundation of church life. With the nurture and support factor of home groups, empowered by the Holy Spirit, Christianity grew dramatically. Nero, a first century Roman Emperor, was alarmed by this phenomenon and declared Christianity illegal, stating that Christians could not build churches or other public meeting places. [1] Violators who attempted to worship Jesus publicly would lose their property, Roman citizenship, and possibly their lives.

Nero kept his promise and became known as a relentless persecutor. He set fire to a city so as to watch its buildings and people burn, and then blamed it on the Christians. [2] He had animal skins sewn around Christians who refused to denounce their faith, and as cheering spectators watched, the martyrs were ripped to pieces by wild dogs. [3] Nero's fame as a persecutor, however, was assured when he became the first emperor to ride a chariot through his private gardens by the light of human torches! He had the Christian martyrs covered with oily tar, and then set on fire for his enjoyment. [4]

Nero's decree lasted some 250 years (A.D. 64-313), but because of home group meetings, the church continued to grow. [5]

An example of the continuation of Nero's decree is seen in the activities of Trajan, the Roman Emperor from 98 to 117 A.D. Trajan revived rigid laws against secret societies. Included in his list was Christianity which he labeled a "depraved and immoderate superstition." Consequently, persecution continued for the Christians who met and worshiped together. [6]

The strength of the Christian home church during this time was illustrated by an incident in A.D. 170. The Roman emperor issued a decree that Christians in Alexandria were to "desist from their faith and meetings" or Roman armies would be sent to destroy them. The bishop of Alexandria (the largest city in Egypt at that time) responded by stating that in order to destroy the Christians, more than half the city's population would have to be executed. [7]

The Christian church continued to flourish in the Roman Empire. There is but one historical reference to a building for Christian gatherings prior to A.D. 300, and that was in Persia in A.D. 265, not the Roman Empire. [8]

By the fourth century, the Roman emperor Constantine, realized that Nero's order of A.D. 64 was unrealistic. Early in his reign he declared Christianity as the official religion of the Roman Empire. This decree resulted in church building projects throughout the empire. With religion and government headquartered in Rome, church and state leaders joined hands to promote the growth of Christianity.

The steps leading to Constantine's decree began in 311 A.D. in the city of Nicomedia by the Roman Emperor Galerius. Galerius declared, "that the purpose of reclaiming the Christians from their willful innovation and the multitude of their sects to the laws and the discipline of Roman State, was not accomplished; and that he would now grant them permission to hold their religious assemblies, provided they disturbed not the order of the state. [9]

Constantine's decree in 313 A.D. went beyond Galerius' decree. It was a decisive step from hostile neutrality to friendly neutrality and protection. It prepared the way for Christianity to be the legally recognized religion of the Roman Empire. The decree ordered the full restoration of all confiscated church property at the expense of the Roman Treasury, and was to be carried out at once! [10]

Constantine, following his decree, led the way in building church structures with elaborate architecture. He immediately built magnificent churches in Jerusalem, Bethlehem, and Constantinople.

Eusebius, an early church historian, describes a church built in Tyre between 313 and 322 A.D. He states it included a large porch, a quadrangular atrium surrounded by columns, a fountain in the center of the atrium for those attending to wash their hands and feet before entering, interior porticoes, galleries, altars, thrones for the bishops, and benches for the church members. Building materials included cedar of Lebanon, granite, and other precious materials. [11]

History reveals the negative effect that church/state alliances and institutionalism had upon the church. The decline in numerical and spiritual growth characterizing this period is remembered today as the Dark Ages.

During the Dark Ages the church's spiritual fellowship and sense of community were exchanged for buildings, ritual, and formality. The house meeting was virtually lost as the medium of spiritual life.

With the blossoming of the Reformation through Martin Luther, Ulrich Zwingli, John Calvin, and other Christian change agents, small groups began to revive.

As Reformers identified the inaccuracy and deception of spiritual leaders concerning Scripture, interest in God's Word grew.

The Gutenberg Bible (first Bible printed with movable type) exploded off the press in 1456, inaugurating a printing revolution that would deliver the Bible from clerical confinement to the eager hands of the common people. The reading of the Scriptures became an exciting event as small groups gathered around the evening fire and studied together. This sparked a resurgence of spirituality in the lives of Christians.

Following the Reformation, Christianity continued to enjoy popular acceptance, but church institutional formality returned. In its wake, home group meetings withered. The influence of Christianity declined in the face of the European Industrial Revolution.

In spite of the religious decline from 1700 through the 1800s, hope continued to flicker. In England, John Wesley and George Whitefield were used by God to spearhead a spiritual revival.

Wesley and Whitefield traveled the English countryside, calling their countrymen back to God. As individuals made decisions for Christ, they were organized into societies. These societies met together in rented facilities for prayer, Bible study, fellowship, and worship. [12]

In Bristol, England, a problem arose in various societies concerning how to raise the money to pay their monthly rent for public meeting places. Consequently, Wesley divided the societies into groups of 12 individuals. He assigned a leader in each group to collect a penny weekly from each family to pay the rent.

As the leaders collected the pennies they reported back to Wesley that they discovered drinking problems, marriage difficulties, and other situations that shouldn't be a part of the Christian lifestyle.

Following this revelation, the collection plan was revised. Wesley suggested, "Why don't we arrange it differently? Why not have the 12 of each group come to one house and there, together, meet and discuss your personal problems. If someone has a problem in his or her life that the group can work out together, then you can share these problems at that time. Also, you can make the collection on that night and save yourselves going from house to house." [13]

The spiritual and personal growth in the lives of the society group members was phenomenal. Word of the positive influence of the Bristol societies traveled to London. Within a short period of time the London society divided into groups of 12. Out of this simple beginning came the Methodist class meetings. These class meetings were home Bible study groups providing Bible study, prayer, and fellowship. Special instructions were given that if a group ever exceeded 12 members, it must divide and begin another group. It was from this group process that the Wesleyan revival in England flourished. It was a revival led by laymen, not clergy—laymen opening the Bible in homes all across England.

Wesley's Methodist movement in England eventually jumped the Atlantic to the United States. The small home Bible study groups caused Methodism to travel very quickly throughout the United States. Churches were built, and public meetings combined with small groups to provide the basis for the growth of Methodism in the United States. [14]

The impact of the small group movement in Methodism also affected the Seventh-day Adventist Church in a unique way. Ellen White was raised a Methodist. Consequently, she observed and was probably aware of small groups in the Methodist Church. At an early age she became involved in the Millerite Movement and the subsequent formation of the Seventh-day Adventist Church. [15]

Early in her leadership experience Ellen White recognized the positive spiritual benefits and numerical growth available through small group ministry. Consequently, she penned the following statements under the direction of God.

"Preach less, and educate more, by holding Bible readings, and by praying with families and little companies." "To all who are working with Christ I would say, Wherever you can gain access to the people by the fireside, improve your opportunity. Take your Bible, and open before them its great truths. Your success will not depend so much upon your knowledge and accomplishments, as upon your ability to find your way to the heart. By being social and coming close to the people, you may turn the current of their thoughts more readily than by the most able discourse. The presentation of Christ in the family, by the fireside, and in small gatherings in private houses is often more successful in winning souls to Jesus than are sermons delivered in the open air, to the moving throng, or even in halls or churches." [16]

"Let small companies assemble together in the evening or early morning to study the Bible for themselves. Let them have a season of prayer that they may be strengthened and enlightened and sanctified by the Holy Spirit. . . . If you will do this, a great blessing will come to you from the One who gave His whole life to service, the One who redeemed you by His own life . . . What testimonies you should bear of the loving acquaintance you have made with your fellow workers in these precious seasons when seeking the blessing of God. Let each tell his experience in simple words. . . . Let little companies meet together to study the Scriptures. You will lose nothing by this, but will gain much" [17]

Ellen White had another opportunity to observe the impact of small groups upon a country and a city. From 1891 to 1900 Ellen White was in Australia assisting with the development of the Seventh-day Adventist Church. While in Australia she assisted in the establishment of Avondale College and wrote several books (The Desire of Ages and Steps to Christ were completed there) that have impacted the Adventist Church.

I believe God placed Ellen White in Australia for another reason that had last-day significance. Ellen White had already experienced firsthand the small group movement in the Methodist Church. God had already revealed to her the importance of small group meetings. Now God was about to reveal to her the potential of the Holy Spirit in small group movements. God was going to give Ellen White a bird's-eye view of what He desired to do through His church prior to the second coming of Jesus to the earth.

During the 1890s in Australia, the exact time of Ellen White's ministry there, events took place that contributed to what is known to us as the Welsh Revival. The Welsh Revival took place when the clergy in and around Melbourne met together to pray for the spiritual health of their members and countrymen. The pastors gained so much strength from this time together that they believed that the best thing they could do for their members' well-being was to organize them into similar groups for Bible study, prayer, and fellowship. Consequently, in the city of Melbourne 2,000 home meetings were occurring weekly at the peak of the revival.

The Melbourne pastors involved in small group ministry invited R. A. Torrey, from the United States of America, to come and conduct an evangelistic campaign. The result was a tremendous revival.

A young woman was visiting Melbourne at this time from Wales. Taking her spiritual experience back to Wales, she assisted in what are called the Cottage Prayer Meetings of

Wales. The cottage meetings contributed to the Welsh Revival which had a tremendous impact on the development and growth of Christianity in Wales. [18]

During this same time period that impacted the Christian church in Australia, God emphasized to Ellen White, during times of prayer and subsequent revelations, the importance of small group ministry. The *Australasian Union Conference Record* of August 15, 1902, recorded the following message:

"The formation of small companies as a basis of Christian effort is a plan that has been presented before me by One who cannot err. If there is a large number in the church, let the members be formed into small companies, to work not only for the church members but for unbelievers also." [19]

"But on such occasions as our annual camp meetings we must never lose sight of the opportunities afforded for teaching the believers how to do practical missionary work in the place where they may live. In many instances it would be well to set apart certain men to carry the burden of different lines of educational work at these meetings. Let some help the people to learn how to give Bible readings and to conduct cottage meetings. Let others bear the burden of teaching the people how to practice the principles of health and temperance, and how to give treatments to the sick. Still others may labor in the interests of our periodical and book work." [20]

"Let the teachers in our schools devote Sunday to missionary effort. Let them take the students with them to hold meetings for those who know not the truth. Sunday can be used for carrying forward various lines of work that will accomplish much for the Lord. On this day house-to-house work can be done. Open-air meetings and cottage meetings can be held." [21]

Small Groups and Twentieth-Century Adventists

As can be seen through history and the pen of Ellen White, God has eternal purposes in mind through small groups. As God revealed events to occur preceding the second coming of Jesus, small groups and sharing the Scriptures with neighbors is an important part of God's plan. The following comments are very convincing.

"In visions of the night, representations passed before me of a great reformatory movement among God's people. Many were praising God. The sick were healed, and other miracles were wrought. A spirit of intercession was seen, even as was manifested before the great Day of Pentecost. Hundreds and thousands were seen visiting families and opening before them the Word of God. Hearts were convicted by the power of the Holy Spirit, and a spirit of genuine conversion was manifest. On every side doors were thrown open to the proclamation of the truth. The world seemed to be lightened with the heavenly influence. Great blessings were received by the true and humble people of God. I heard voices of thanksgiving and praise, and there seemed to be a reformation such as we witnessed in 1844."[22]

The question comes, If small groups (Home Bible Study groups, cottage meetings, Tender Loving Care groups [TLCs], Homes of Hope, or whatever term a person chooses to use) are God-inspired, then why is there resistance among some Protestant members, including some Seventh-day Adventists, toward small groups?

The reasons, of course, are varied. Some individuals believe that small groups are only therapy groups. Others, that it is a seedbed for nonsupportive independent denominational splinter groups. Some feel groups may fragment the congregation into cliques. Also, a number of individuals are more introverted in personality and are afraid they will have to "open up" and express their opinions or feelings about a particular topic to the extent that they become uncomfortable.

However, the question that arises the most among SDAs is based on the unfounded premise that small groups is a program developed in the 1980s and used by other Protestant churches. The question asked is "Why must the SDA Church adopt programs from other Protestant churches?" The preceding historical information, however, reveals that small group ministries are one of God's methods of evangelism and a significant tool in the final days of Earth's history. I imagine Satan is excited. He has placed a veil over a significant portion of God's end-time strategy in the Seventh-day Adventist Church. Not only are small outreach groups to be used in every community to teach biblical truth, but during the final closing events of this earth's history, when SDA Christians are scattered, small groups will be the norm, not the unusual! Adventists will appreciate the company of their group.

"I saw the saints leaving the cities and villages, and associating together in companies, and living in the most solitary places. Angels provided them food and water, while the wicked were suffering from hunger and thirst." [23]

Adventist Small Groups—1980s and 1990s

During the 1960s and 1970s numerous Seventh-day Adventist congregations began small group ministries. Most of these ministries were Christian nurture/Bible study groups. The mission focus of outreach, for the most part, was missing.

Emphasis, however, in regard to the importance of small groups as having evangelistic potential was seen in 1986 with the development of new lessons in Texas. Revelation Seminars Unlimited printed a set of Home Series Revelation lessons, designed for home seminar use. These lessons utilized traditional teaching methods more than the group/discovery methodology.

A further development also took place in 1986. Under the leadership of Garrie Williams, ministerial director of the Oregon Conference, steps were taken that began a nurture/outreach small group movement across North America and spilled over into the rest of the world.

During the fall of 1986 through early 1987 an Adventist awareness program consisting of television, radio, and newspaper ads concerning the Seventh-day Adventist Church's beliefs and doctrines culminated in conference-wide Revelation seminars.

Beginning March 2, 1988, 228 seminars began throughout the conference. Virtually every Oregon church conducted a seminar. Approximately 700 church members formed leadership teams.

At the conclusion of the seminars an interesting discovery took place. Of the 228 seminars, 50 were conducted in homes. These 50 produced a higher percentage of baptisms and attendance than the seminars held in public buildings or churches. Further analysis revealed that the relationships formed in the small group (3-12 individuals) made the difference. With this discovery in mind, new lessons for "relational Bible study" were written, members were trained, and the Home Bible Study format was born in Oregon.

A total of 2,000 small groups (Neighborhood Home Bible Studies/Homes of Hope) were planned, utilizing the new relational inductive Bible Study lessons. These materials were on the books of Revelation and John.

Two rallies—one in Portland, Oregon, and the other in Grants Pass, Oregon—combined with fasting and prayer, prepared the way for the 800 home fellowship groups that began in March 1988.

More than 2,000 church members teamed together to lead the 800 groups, while another 2,400 church members participated as group members.

Non-Adventist attendance averaged 2 to 3 per group. Some groups had no non-SDA members, while others had 5 or 6 in attendance.

At the close of 1988, 1,239 Homes of Hope had functioned in Oregon, with another 776 in the North American Division and overseas, making a total of 15 beyond the target of 2,000. By the end of 1989 approximately 700 individuals had been baptized as a direct result or through related contact with small group ministry. To date about 50 percent of Oregon's 120 churches continue with small group ministry.

God desires to pour out the Holy Spirit in latter-rain proportions upon His church and, in so doing, empower Bible study groups. These groups have a significant place in the

Seventh-day Adventist Church's mission and outreach methodologies. The question is Are Seventh-day Adventists ignoring God's method as Protestant Christianity carries the torch?

---

[1] Philip Schaff, *History of the Christian Church.* (Grand Rapids, Mich.: Eerdman's Pub. Co., 1959), vol. 1, p. 384.

[2] *Ibid.,* p. 379.

[3] *Ibid.,* p. 382.

[4] *Ibid.*

[5] *Ibid.,* and vol. 2, p. 274.

[6] *Ibid.,* vol. 2, p. 46.

[7] Albert J. Wollen, *Miracles Happen in Group Bible Study* (Glendale, California: Regal Books, G. L. Publications, 1976), p. 29.

[8] *Ibid.,* p. 30.

[9] Schaff, vol. 2, p. 71.

[10] *Ibid.,* p. 72.

[11] *Ibid.,* pp. 198-202.

[12] John Dillenberger and Claude Welch, *Protestant Christianity* (New York: Charles Scribner and Sons, 1954), pp. 129-136.

[13] B. Waugh and T. Mason, *The Works of the Reverend John Wesley,* (1832), vol. 7, p. 12.

[14] Wollen, p. 36.

[15] Arthur W. Spalding, *Origin and History of Seventh-day Adventists,* (Washington, D.C.: Review and Herald Pub. Assn., 1961), vol. 1, p. 61.

[16] Ellen G. White, *Gospel Workers* (Washington, D.C.: Review and Herald Pub. Assn., 1948), p. 193.

[17] _____, *This Day With God* (Washington, D.C.: Review and Herald Pub. Assn., 1979), p. 11.

[18] Wollen, pp. 36, 37.

[19] Quoted in Ellen G. White, *Evangelism* (Washington, D.C.: Review and Herald Pub. Assn., 1946), p. 115.

[20] _____, *Testimonies for the Church* (Mountain View, Calif.: Pacific Press Pub. Assn., 1948), vol. 9, pp. 82, 83.

[21] _____, *Counsels to Parents and Teachers* (Mountain View, Calif.: Pacific Press Pub. Assn., 1913), p. 551.

[22] _____, *Testimonies,* vol. 9, p. 126.

[23] _____, *Early Writings* (Washington, D.C.: Review and Herald Pub. Assn., 1882), p. 282.

C H A P T E R
3

Introduction to Small Groups

Recently I assisted with a national small group seminar on the West Coast. Two days into the seminar I was approached by a gentleman named Dave. He said, "I have come to this seminar with no background in small group ministry. I have never listened to a cassette tape or read a book explaining small group philosophy and principles, and have never participated in a group. I want to go home with four questions answered. First, what is a small group? Second, what are the various types of groups? Third, how does an outreach group differ from other types of groups? And fourth, how do you start a group?"

Dave's questions are basic to understanding small group ministry. Because of their significance, let's examine them closely.

Definition of a Small Group

In attempting to define small groups, remember that small group is a technical term referring to interpersonal dynamics within the group, not necessarily its size. However, as used in local church ministry, a small group definition will include numbers of people present.

The following diagrams illustrate this concept. [1] Although diagrams A and B are not small groups numerically, many small group principles apply to them. If the leader's style and approach in A and B are more inductive/relational than deductive/instructional, the meetings will have a small group flavor.

A. Sermon preaching, public evangelism, lecturing

B. Teaching, seminars, instructional classes

C. Small group, relational dynamic

A definition used widely in Protestant churches today is as follows: A small group is an intentional, face-to-face gathering of 3-12 people, on a regular time schedule, with the common purpose of discovering and growing in the abundant life of Christ. [2]

However, for the purpose of small group evangelism I have adapted the definition to be:

A small group is an intentional, face-to-face gathering of 3-12 people, on a regular time schedule, with the common purpose of discovering biblical truth, of growing in the abundant life in Jesus Christ, and of leading others to accept Jesus as Lord and Saviour of their lives.

The major difference between an outreach small group and a task or nurture group is that the outreach group's major time commitment is dedicated to their outreach mission.

Types of Groups

All Christian small groups are not the same. Invariably, when someone mentions the term *small groups,* red flags arise for those who remember the encounter groups of the 1960s and 1970s. However, the confrontational group styles of the recent past have nothing in common with Christian small groups. Christian groups exist for the sole purpose of uplifting Jesus Christ and modeling Him to the group members.

The following are the most common types of small

groups.[3]

1. *Sharing/Prayer Group.* The emphasis is on sharing what God is doing in the lives of group members. Daily concerns are shared as the group prays for answers and seeks the power of the Holy Spirit for their personal lives and the church.

2. *Bible Study Group.* The emphasis is on studying Scripture. Although the ingredients of fellowship and prayer exist, they are not the main focus of the group. The group's major concern is understanding Scripture from an inductive approach and its application to daily Christian living.

3. *Nurture (Covenant) Group.* The covenant and Bible study groups both have fellowship, Bible study, sharing, and prayer. The significant difference is that the covenant group focuses upon fellowship. This is an excellent group for discipling newly baptized church members or recent transfers from another church.

4. *Support Group.* A support group is established for the purpose of assisting individuals with similar felt needs to find healing, love, and friendship. Examples of felt needs are divorce, single parenting, death, drug abuse, alcohol recovery, overcoming tobacco usage, etc.

5. *Outreach (Mission) Group.* The emphasis involves using members' spiritual gifts for the building up of the body of Christ numerically and spiritually. Outreach groups are usually Bible study-oriented or project-oriented.

6. *House Church.* A group of people who meet in a home rather than a church building. All dynamics of a large church are present except for the size of the group and related dynamics.

Models of Outreach Groups

Although there are various kinds of outreach groups, the goal is the same: to lead individuals to make a decision to accept Jesus as Lord and Saviour of their lives and to apply biblical knowledge to daily living.

Home Bible Study Groups

In 1987 the Oregon Conference of Seventh-day Adventists developed a group Bible study program entitled Homes of Hope. The program involves church members inviting neighbors and other acquaintances to their homes for a Bible study. Groups consist of 3 to 12 individuals of various faiths studying a particular book or passage of the Bible together in order to discover a correct understanding of Scripture and its application to daily life.

The study lessons developed and used most often in Oregon are on the book of John and the book of Revelation. Other lessons utilizing the inductive study method are also applicable to this type of setting.

The Home Bible Study method utilizes the principles of small groups and closely adheres to the principles of fellowship, prayer, nurture, and discipleship found in other types of groups.

Project Groups

These could also be called clubs or task groups. Members participate because they are interested in a similar task. It might be literature distribution, giving individual home Bible studies, mailing literature to missionaries, hospital visitation, visiting former members, presenting health awareness seminars, etc.

The group meets once every week or two, briefly studying a passage of Scripture. They pray, share experiences from their outreach, encourage one another, and plan future projects.

The group members then collectively, individually, or as pairs (according to their schedule) conduct that particular outreach project.

The Mt. Tabor Seventh-day Adventist Church in Portland, Oregon, has developed project groups which are fulfilling the central part of the church's outreach ministry.

Home Evangelistic Groups

Miguel Cerna, pastor of the Norwalk Spanish church in Norwalk, California, and vice president of the Southern California Conference, has developed this group strategy very successfully. In a seven-year period, Pastor Cerna has seen more than 1,000 individuals baptized through the efforts of his church members.

What do the members do? Every member is organized into a group. They visit their friends, neighbors, media interests, and other sources of names and invite them to take Bible studies. When an individual accepts the invitation, the member returns on a weekly basis and conducts the individual study.

When the individuals progress to a point where they are interested in a group study, they are placed in a group. Each group consists of individuals like themselves who have been studying weekly. Students and their instructors form a group of 8 to 12 people. A reaping series of printed lessons or filmstrips are used in the home setting to assist in preparing the individuals for baptism. This is followed up yearly by the Pastor conducting an evangelistic series.

This small group method utilizes both traditional teaching methods and the group/discovery methodology. Pastor Cerna is currently writing a book on this successful approach.

Sabbath School Action Groups

Several pastors have used, with success, an adapted small group method with the Sabbath School class. The approach varies, but a basic principle prevails—the Sabbath school class is a natural weekly study opportunity. So let's use it to greater advantage as a nurture and outreach tool.

The classes are kept to a maximum of 12 members. The class time is divided into several segments. These are sharing, planning outreach, Bible study, and prayer. The group members not only spend time studying the Sabbath school lesson together, but they share their personal concerns. The members support each other and pray for one another.

The class also chooses one or more outreach projects. It may be feeding the homeless, giving Bible studies, conducting a small group home Bible study or a Revelation Seminar, literature distribution, visitation, or assisting a person in need. The list is endless. The class members decide when and how often to meet or participate in the outreach activity.

The Michigan Conference church ministries' leaders have developed this approach in an excellent manner.

An excellent approach is to have each Sabbath school class conduct a weekly home outreach small group. The non-SDA members attending the group have a natural connection to the church. The group leader can invite non-SDAs to the Sabbath school class that several of the home group members attend. The non-SDA has friends in both the home and church who love them and help them feel needed and welcome.

This is an excellent outreach, nurture, and church assimilation method.

All of the group outreach methods discussed are excellent and effective. But of all the methods, the one that follows closest to the small group principles of inductive Bible study is the Home Bible Study Group.

The Home Bible Study method also contains elements of nurture and support that provides for complete discipling of the new and established Christian. As a result, the major focus of this book is on how to start and develop Home Bible Study groups in the local church setting.

Worship/Subgroups/Small Groups

It is obvious to the observer of growing churches that small group ministry is a key ingredient. It is not the only ingredient, but it is a vital part of a vibrant church. Analyzing the healthy church, we discover that it is made up of three factors: an uplifting worship service, subgroups, and small groups.

The *worship service* involves the entire church membership. Worship is experienced as a united church body each Sabbath morning.

The *subgroup* consists of more than 12 individuals who are involved in some activity not involving the entire membership. This could be the choir, Pathfinders, singles, young adults, large Sabbath school classes, etc.

The *small* group consists of 12 or less members who form a special relationship with each other. It not only involves specific activities (e.g., outreach, Bible study, etc.), but the group develops close friendships—sharing the joys and frustrations of life with one another. The members can pray, study, cry, laugh, eat, and shop together!

In other words, the small group members care and love one another through one-to-one fellowship that is not possible in a large group setting.

No matter how small or large your church membership may be, small groups are essential to its health. Some individuals who state that churches with large memberships cannot be loving and caring overlook the small group factor. A church of 10,000 members with a healthy small group ministry can be more loving and caring than a church of 50 members who have shallow relationships with one another.

Church growth experts have discovered an essential fact for maintaining healthy church members: Each member needs a minimum of seven individuals whom he or she considers their friends. Each person also needs someone, preferably more than one, who is considered a special friend. Studies indicate that if this doesn't occur, the member runs a higher risk of not attending church. [4]

Further studies demonstrate that in most churches, including Seventh-day Adventist churches, friendliness and a feeling of being loved are more significant than doctrine, in keeping members attending.

A study was conducted by Des Cummings, Jr., and Roger Dudley at Andrews University (Berrien Springs, Michigan), concerning nonattending members in one Northwest SDA conference. This survey revealed that a large percentage of the nonattending members believed friendliness would have kept them attending church, and would be a significant factor in their return.[5] Small group church ministry is a vital resource in meeting this need.

---

[1] Garrie F. Williams, *Trinity Power Circle* (Clackamas, Oreg.: Neighborhood Home Bible Study, 1989), p. 40A.

[2] Roberta Hestenes, *Class Lectures* (Pasadena, Calif.: Fuller Theological Seminary Pasadena, 1986).

[3] Skip Bell, *Together in Christ* (Grants Pass, Oreg.).

[4] Win Arn, *The Win Arn Growth Report,* Number 8, 1985 (709 E. Colorado Blvd., Suite 150, Pasadena, Calif. 91101).

[5] Roger Dudley and Des Cummings, Jr., *Adventures in Church Growth* (Hagerstown, Md., Review and Herald Pub. Assn., 1983), pp. 146, 147.

CHAPTER
4

Four Components of Small Groups

In 1948 China was convulsed by civil war. City after city fell to the Communists, who were sweeping down from the north. The war and great floods had left approximately 55 million Chinese homeless. Prices were skyrocketing. Famine threatened. If anyone had an excuse to not worry about the preaching of the Word, it was the Chinese, who were devoting major amounts of time and energy just attempting to survive.

However, sensing the shortness of the hour, SDA missionaries and Chinese nationals launched Mission 48 on April 4, 1948, with 50 public meetings. The outreach, however, closed down very quickly. On December 9, 1948, a telegram was received by the General Conference: "Evacuating missionaries from north and central to south China." Early in 1949 the last American Adventist missionaries were evacuated from mainland China.

Between 1949 and 1950 the official work of the church in China was slowly winding down. Beginning in 1951, native SDA church leaders were feeling the pressure by the Communists to close the work in China completely. By 1966 China's Red Guard had virtually wiped out what was left of the open Christian witness. Following were the silent years. [1]

In recent years, with great anticipation, Christians of all denominations have wondered how Christianity fared during that period. Had Christianity been able to survive the expulsion of missionaries, the shutdown of churches, and harsh persecution? Not only had churches survived, but they had grown dramatically![2]

The Chinese Christian church grew significantly during the time of spiritual oppression. How was this possible? Home fellowship groups is the answer.

Christians in China had met in small, informal home gatherings for worship, prayer, and Bible study. In this support setting they found faith, courage, strength, and hope to continue in the Christian faith.[3]

In 1976 the Chinese government began to relax its control in many places, and the Christian work began to revive. Even though many Christian leaders were still in prison in 1977 and 1978, the house church movement accelerated.

Beginning in 1979, the government gradually permitted churches to reopen. Today, approximately 5,000 churches are open. Protestant church buildings accommodate about 5 million each week, with numerous others meeting in homes.

In fact, the majority of Christians in China today meet where services are conducted in homes. The estimated number of Chinese Christians attending house churches ranges from a few million to 50 million. Conservative sources estimate that 20 to 30 million is a realistic number.

In the rural areas of China the house church is flourishing rapidly. The Adventist Church has enjoyed nearly a tenfold increase—from a few thousand to 65,000 in the past ten years.[4]

A tribute to the advancement of Christianity in China was achieved in 1988 when Amity Press in Nanjing, China, printed the one millionth copy of the Chinese Bible. Scripture in the hands and homes of Chinese Christians will ensure the further growth of Christianity.[5]

This is only one example of the Holy Spirit's power working through groups providing nurture and outreach. Similar stories concerning groups could be told from Latin America, Britain, the United States, Korea, and other countries around the earth. These contemporary stories echo the experience of the Waldenses during the Middle Ages.

The Waldensian people, through home group meetings,

were faithful to God and evangelized, even though their crops, homes, and churches were destroyed. The blood of their martyrs watered the gospel seed and yielded decisions for Christ centuries before even Martin Luther's time.[6]

Today Christian small groups can still meet some of the basic interpersonal needs that were met in centuries past. These needs include:

- friendship, support, and encouragement.
- giving and receiving love.
- strength to deal with the negative issues of life.
- serving others.
- a sense of "belonging."
- spiritual growth.

These basic interpersonal needs can be satisfied by the four components of small groups found in Acts 2:42-47. The components are

(1) nurture,
(2) worship,
(3) community,
(4) mission.[7]

"And they continued steadfastly in the apostles' doctrine and fellowship, in the breaking of bread, and in prayers. Then fear came upon every soul, and many wonders and signs were done through the apostles. Now all who believed were together, and had all things in common, and sold their possessions and goods, and divided them among all, as anyone had need. So continuing daily with one accord in the temple, and breaking bread from house to house, they ate their food with gladness and simplicity of heart, praising God and having favor with all the people. And the Lord added to the church daily those who were being saved" (Acts 2:42-47, NKJV).

1. **Nurture.** The new believers devoted themselves to the apostles' teaching. Today we would say that those who believed in Jesus studied the Bible and applied that which they learned to their lives, including love and support of one another.

Not only is Bible study primary in Christian living, but

fellowship of friend with friend is a key ingredient as well. Win Arn, of the Institute of Church Growth, Pasadena, California, after interviewing 100 new members (50 were currently active and 50 had stopped attending), discovered the importance of fellowship and friendship. [8]

The results were as follows:

Number of New Friends in the Church	0	1	2	3	4	5	6	7	8	9+
Actives	0	0	0	1	2	2	8	13	12	12
Drop-outs	8	13	14	8	4	2	1	0	0	0

Look at the difference! In the group of 50 active members, 8 had made 6 new friends, 13 had made 7 new friends, 12 had made 8 new friends, and 12 had made 9 or more new friends.

What a contrast to the inactive members. Eight of the 50 could identify no new friends made in the first six months, 13 could list only one; 14 made 2 new friends. None of the members in this group had made any more than 6 new friends. The result? They dropped out! [9]

Like the early church, friendships formed through studying God's Word together will have a bonding of man to God and man to man through the working of the Holy Spirit. This time together will lead to worshiping God and willing obedience to what He commands.

2. **Worship**—the second component of small groups in the early church. The natural response to the study of God's Word is praise and joy. Acts 2:46, 47 states that when the people saw all that God had done for them, they praised God with a sincere heart. This sincerity bonded them together in oneness for corporate worship and adoration of God.

3. **Community.** Nurture and worship, when practiced in openness and forthrightness, brings the members together in community. It means that a group of people hold specific items in common. This commonality brings oneness, which

also prepares for the vital working of the Holy Spirit. Some of the items shared together in a small group are:

- sharing in God's grace in Christ (Phil. 1:7).
- being united with Christ in His death, resurrection, and glory (Rom. 6:3, 4).
- elevated to the position of sons and daughters of God (John 1:12).
- recognizing a group member's need, and being willing to meet that need (Acts 2:44, 45).
- "being of one heart and soul" (Acts 4:32).

It is no wonder that some of the criticisms leveled toward early church Christians were slanderous in nature, based on jealousy concerning how they loved one another. Yes, the greatest evidence of true Christianity is a helpful and loving Christian.

4. **Mission.** A group of individuals sharing together in nurture, worship, and community will not be legitimate in their existence if they remain inward. This is a biblical principle.

The reason that some groups fail—the reason that groups that exist only for nurture, worship, and community stagnate and die is that Christians must share with others outside of the group that which they have discovered in Christ, or they are not complete. There will be no *bottom line* reason for the group's existence. This is a vital Biblical principle. Jesus said, "The Son of Man also came not to be served but to serve" (Mark 10:45). Paul aptly understood this principle when he said: "Do not forget to do good and to share with others, for with such sacrifices God is pleased" (Heb. 13:16, NIV).

When the Christian, made in the image of Jesus, follows His example, the small group will never become closed, a clique, or without outreach. The group will not only share with each other, but will reach out together meeting the needs of others while keeping in mind the goal of enlarging their group.

The mission of the small groups mentioned in Acts 2 (to call others to Jesus Christ) had remarkable results. "The Lord added to the church daily those who were being saved" (Acts 2:47, NKJV).

The rapid growth resulted because of two characteristics being present. First, the believers, as we have seen, had a common bond or oneness in Jesus Christ—to Him and one another. This meant that when those on the outside looked in, they saw that these group members loved God, loved one another, and loved those not yet of the group. Jesus said remarkable things happen when these factors are present. "By this all will know that you are My disciples, if you have love for one another" (John 13:35, NKJV).

Second, because the Christians were one with God and one another, the Holy Spirit worked through them in the power of Pentecost. As one writer has so aptly summarized: "The church is consciously inadequate persons who gather because they are weak, and scatter to serve because unity with each other and Christ has made them bold." [10]

Ellen White predicts the same for our day when the identical components are experienced. "To us today, as verily as to the first disciples, the promise of the Spirit belongs. God will today endow men and women with power from above, as He endowed those who on the Day of Pentecost heard the word of salvation. At this very hour His Spirit and His grace are for all who need them and will take Him at His word." [11]

---

[1] Roland Hegstad, Religious Liberty Sermon. Oregon Pastor's Conference, January 1972.

[2] Roberta Hestenes, *Using the Bible in Groups* (Philadelphia, Pa.: Westminster Press, 1983), p. 9.

[3] *Ibid.,* p. 10.

[4] Samuel C. Young, in *Adventist Review,* Sept. 7, 1989, p. 12.

[5] *Adventist Review,* Nov. 30, 1989.

[6] Ellen G. White, *The Great Controversy* (Mountain View, Calif.: Pacific Press Pub. Assn., 1911), pp. 75, 76.

[7] Steve Barker, Judy Johnson, Jenny Long, Rob Malone, and Ron Nicholas, *Small Group Leader's Handbook* (Downers Grove, Ill.: InterVarsity Press, 1982), pp. 29, 30.

[8] Win Arn, Charles Arn, and Carol Nyquist, *Who Cares About Love?* (Pasadena, Calif.: Church Growth Press, 1986), p. 180.

[9] *Ibid.,* p. 180.

[10] Barker, p. 32.

[11] White, *Testimonies,* vol. 8, p. 20.

CHAPTER

5

A Small Group Is Different

The small group Bible study fellowship approach has some differences from the classroom style of study. Some of these differences are:

1. The meeting is in a home rather than the church or public building.

2. The seating arrangement is with chairs in a circle rather than in rows.

3. Group meetings are usually one night per week, one and a half to two hours long.

4. Rather than a prepared lecture by a teacher, there is a leader-guided Bible study and discussion.

5. The lesson focuses on interpersonal relationships, biblical understanding, and application of biblical knowledge.

6. Care is taken to not give heavy doctrinal material before the group members are ready. Follow-up groups and classes are usually needed to present all doctrines and instruction.

7. Decisions are called for throughout the lessons, but not to the point of producing pressure that would cause some to stop attending.

8. The maximum number of participants in a small group should be approximately 12, in contrast to a class lecture style accommodating any number.

The premise of the small group approach is that it is only the first step for many individuals in their walk with God. Hopefully this initiates a chain of continued contacts with the group members as they progress toward a fulfilling relationship with God and the church.

The apostle Paul in 1 Corinthians 3:1, 2 stated: "Brothers, I could not address you as spiritual but as worldly—mere infants in Christ. I gave you milk, not solid food, for you were not yet ready for it" (NIV).

Paul recognized that spiritual material needs to be given step-by-step as a person understands the basics. He compared it in this passage to the progression of a baby from mother's milk to solid food. Ellen White reminds us of this principle when she states, "You need not feel that all the truth is to be spoken to unbelievers on any and every occasion. You should plan carefully what to say and what to leave unsaid. This is not practicing deception; it is to work as Paul worked." [1]

Based upon these divinely inspired principles, this statement in *The Ministry of Healing* summarizes the evangelistic strategy of the small group fellowship: "Christ's method alone will give true success in reaching the people. The Saviour mingled with men as one who desired their good. He showed His sympathy for them, ministered to their needs, and won their confidence. Then He bade them, 'Follow Me.'" [2]

What was Christ's method of approaching people? He did not spend most of His time in public meetings. Instead, He met them on their own turf. If they had a need, He met it. If they needed empathy, He empathized. If they needed sympathy, He sympathized. Only when He had established a relationship of confidence based upon a genuine love and friendship did He invite them to accept Him as Lord and Saviour of their life.

Wherever you find Jesus you find Him talking to people, getting acquainted, desiring to relieve their problems and give them salvation. There was Jesus and the woman at the well (John 4), Jesus and Nicodemus (John 3), and Jesus and Simon (John 12). Jesus came together with literally thousands of people because He genuinely cared.

Keep these principles in mind: The *first* agenda item of the small group leader is to become a friend to his individual group members and to win their confidence. If an individual is a stranger to you, you may have only one opportunity to present Christ and His teaching. If you have the person's confidence, then you can approach the subject several times without offending him.

Second, as you study the biblical material, be aware of the personal needs of your members. If, for example, an individual is having marital difficulties, the problems will many times be uppermost in his mind rather than the biblical material. As you empathize with him you should direct his attention to prayer and strength in God. A listening friend will provide healing power by giving support and not necessarily advice. Remember, God uses friendship and love to prepare the receptivity of the heart and mind for spiritual realities.

Third, remember that it is not imperative for members of your group to understand all the details of the biblical material at the same time. The spiritual backgrounds of your members will be diverse. In ministering to others, Jesus realized that fruit ripens at different times.

As a youth I picked citrus fruit in Arizona. When I first began, when the foreman took me out to the orchard, he gave me a large wire ring that clipped to my gloved finger. The ring was a gauge to judge whether the fruit was large enough to be picked. I was also informed concerning the proper coloration of the fruit. The foreman didn't expect the crew to pick all the fruit at the same time. We knew we would be returning later to the same tree to pick the fruit that wasn't ready the first time.

The above illustration leads into the *fourth* major observation. The small group meeting is only a beginning point. After you complete the biblical study guides, you can provide various options for your members to continue growing. These options would include continuing group studies on another Bible book, a pastor's class (group) at Sabbath school, a baptismal/doctrinal group, individual Bible studies on doctrinal subjects, etc.

In some cases the group member may choose not to be involved with further studies. If this is the case, they are still a friend. Continue the relationship through visiting and social settings. The individual may desire to participate further in the future. Genuine love and friendship, however, does not dictate that an individual must accept Christ or Seventh-day Adventism in order for a relationship to be maintained.

---

[1] White, *Evangelism,* p. 125.
[2] _____, *The Ministry of Healing* (Mountain View, Calif.: Pacific Press Pub. Assn., 1942), p. 143.

How Will They Learn?

I was attending a Sabbath school class in the state of Washington. The teacher welcomed every member and visitor in a manner that put each of us at ease. He then said, "We have several types of classes in our church. In my class I do most of the talking and share information and ideas. I invite you to participate, but I have a certain amount of material I want to give you. If any of you prefer more discussion and interchange of ideas and experiences, there is a class that meets in the elders' room. The members sit in a circle and discuss their viewpoints on the Scriptures. If you prefer that type of learning experience, it won't offend me." The teacher then proceeded to give an excellent presentation with minimal verbal class participation.

The teacher unintentionally summarized two basic approaches to sharing knowledge upon a subject—in this case biblical knowledge. The two approaches are the teacher-centered approach (the didactic method), and the student-centered approach (the inductive method).

The didactic method is more instructional. The teacher does as the name implies; he instructs or teaches information. The teacher designs the class outline and decides what to emphasize. The didactic method involves:
- an emphasis on information
- emphasis on how to learn
- learning through participation
- interaction from teacher to student or student to

teacher, not student to student

The following diagram illustrates this methodology.

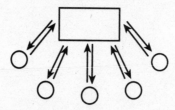

The inductive method, student-centered approach, is discovery learning. The teacher facilitates learning as a group leader rather than as the authority who imparts knowledge. The group leader outlines and prepares information to share, but prefers to help the students discover answers to questions for themselves rather than just tell the answers. This approach focuses upon the student, and provides a process for them to grow by discovering knowledge rather than just receiving the teacher's knowledge.

The inductive method involves:

- An emphasis on the process of individual discovery
- The student deciding what's important to learn
- Teaching through participation
- Interaction from leader to student, student to leader, and student to student.

The following diagram illustrates this methodology.

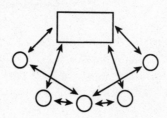

How Do These Methods Work?

The didactic and inductive methods can be applied to teaching Scripture in the following manner.

In the didactic method, the teacher would:

1. *Determine the student's Bible position.*

That is, find out what the student already understands about a biblical topic or topics.

2. *Impart knowledge.*

Once the teacher has determined the student's level of understanding on a topic, the teacher determines what information to teach.

3. *Inspire desire.*

Biblical facts and principles are not only to be learned, but lived as well. The goal of the Bible teacher is to motivate his students as a channel of the Holy Spirit, to apply scriptural principles to their lives.

4. *Generate action*

The teacher makes specific suggestions on how the student can respond to God's Word. The goal is to assist the student in making life-changing decisions.

In the inductive method, the teacher would:

1. *Begin with a basic question.*

After selecting a text or passage of Scripture and identifying the topic for discussion, present questions that stimulate interaction. The student will reveal his knowledge or position on the topic based upon his input in the discussion.

2. *Suggest Resources for Understanding.*

As the discussion and interchange of ideas takes place, the teacher suggests other passages, historical information, commentaries, etc., that might assist the students in discovering the desired answer. The teacher guides the student to the sources of information instead of stating the facts.

3. *Assist students in evaluating.*

Once facts are discovered, the students and teacher will discuss together how these findings impact daily living. Together, they evaluate their conclusions and their viability to current life situations.

4. *Be available to assist students in action.*

Once the student evaluates the information discovered and through group discussion has decided specific action to take in his life, the teacher is available to be of assistance as necessary.

As one can see, both the inductive and didactic methods have some similarities and both possess the same goal. It is the approach to the goal that is different. In some outreach group settings there will be a blending of the two approaches. However, most types of groups will use the inductive approach. In groups that use the inductive method the teacher is called a "leader." The student is called a group "member."

Getting Started

Once an individual decides to initiate a home Bible study outreach group, the person naturally asks, "How do I start?" To answer this question, five areas will be discussed: the host home, the group leader, the assistant leader, the host or hostess, and the study materials.

It would be helpful for the person beginning a Bible study outreach group to have several individuals assist them. However, one person can do it alone, but if at all possible, have at least two people involved. The number of individuals assisting will determine how the five basic job functions are divided.

Host Home

The host home is the home that is opened as the location for the study group to meet. It can belong to someone who is not the group leader or host/hostess. It can simply be the residence of an individual who wants to dedicate his home to God as a meeting place. However, the owner of the host home, if possible, should participate in the study group. In one study group in which I was leader, the homeowner would either leave during our meeting or go downstairs and watch television. The group members questioned the homeowner's reluctance to participate. Consequently, an awkward situation developed.

The choice of the room for your study is important. An uncomfortably cold or warm room, noisy children, or pets can distract group members. A wise choice of location is important. Careful planning should provide:

• A comfortable atmosphere around a kitchen table, a family room, or similar location.

• Good lighting, which is necessary to provide for ideal study conditions and a warm atmosphere.

• Arrange seating in a circle so all can see and discuss with each other.

• Guard against distractions. Children, pets, telephones, television, radios, etc., can disrupt your study group. Choose a location that will provide the fewest interruptions.

• In order for some group members to attend, baby-sitting may be necessary. If your home has additional space and a volunteer can be obtained, this is an option to consider.

Group Leader

The group leader's role is essential to the success of the group. The leader needs to be a facilitator of group discussion and personal relationships more than an authority or distributor of information. The Bible study group is not a lecture presentation, but a carefully guided discussion. Because the study focuses on Scripture, the leader will need to provide some direction. However, the personal contribution of each group member serves as an opportunity for the leader to emphasize the scriptural meaning.

A few basic guidelines for the group leader:

• Prayer and spiritual preparation is the first and most important step for a group leader. Through the power of the Holy Spirit, the least experienced individual can be dramatically effective.

• Be enthusiastic about studying the Bible—not only for the theological learning, but for applying it to daily life.

• Understand the passage to be studied. Prayer and Bible study preparation are essential. Don't be sidetracked from this priority. The leader must be fed spiritually in order to share with others and to guide group members through the material.

• Be excited about your group's discoveries in Scripture.

This will encourage them to deeper study. Even if it's not new to you, it's exciting to watch them grow.

• Use illustrations to explain biblical passages, and share how the Scripture applies to daily life. A personal testimony or experience by yourself or fellow group member can be helpful to others.

• Answer questions, and provide necessary resource material. Make sure that group members are visited as needed and that those who make decisions for Jesus Christ are led into a relationship with Him.

• Assist those who desire deeper doctrinal study into SDA Bible beliefs and encourage them to become church members.

• Ensure that the overall needs of the group are being met.

• Have empathy with other group members. Try to, "Walk in their moccasins" for a day. Be genuinely interested in showing love and friendliness.

Caution

In the process of developing your skills as a leader it is easy to become discouraged. There will be tendencies to compare your group with other groups, to become discouraged if members don't return, and to consider yourself a failure if you have what you consider a poor group study. Satan desires you to fail—but God has overcome the evil one! Persevere in faith and prayer, and victory will be yours! Remember to speak, and "do not be afraid, for I am with you" (Acts 18:9, NKJV). God's promise is a promise also for God's present-day spokespersons.

Assistant Leader

There are times when the group leader will not be able to attend a meeting. Because of this, an assistant is needed. The assistant should work closely with the leader in endeavoring to meet the needs of the group members during the time prior to and following group study nights. The assistant should not endeavor to lead the study, but should take care to allow the leader to lead.

The assistant is also a prime candidate to begin a new group in the future. He should understand that it is desirable for the group to increase in attendance. When this occurs, the group should divide and the assistant would be the logical new leader.

The assistant leader is also a prayer partner, encourager, and coevaluator with the leader. The two of them together can be more effective than going it alone. They can discuss what happened in the group and why events occurred as they did. In fact, the assistant may often be able to observe what is happening more clearly because of not being under the pressure of directing the discussion.

Host/Hostess

The host/hostess doesn't necessarily have to live in the home in which the group is meeting. This individual, however, should be a member of the group. As needs arise, the host/hostess can quietly leave the group to fulfill his or her responsibilities.

The responsibilities are:
- Welcome the group members as they arrive.
- Take their coats.
- Make sure the group members' needs are met. Show them the location of the bathroom, drinking glasses, and telephone. Assist in making them relaxed and comfortable.
- Make sure there is adequate seating. If necessary, bring in a chair from another room. The chairs should be in a circle. Do not have some members sitting outside of the circle. Psychologically, this hinders their participation and the group dynamics.
- Take care of distractions. If the telephone rings, the host/hostess should answer it. If the dog gets loose from the laundry room, he becomes the dog catcher. The group leader

should explain to the group that the host/hostess will period-ically leave the group to take care of needs as they arise. Also, the group members can ask the host/hostess to assist them at any time. This might sound formal, but after a few meetings there develops a relaxed routine and atmosphere.

• Smile, be friendly, and show genuine concern.

• Provide name tags at the first few meetings if your group is large.

Bible Study Materials

There are various options available for group Bible study. The group leader should choose a subject the members are comfortable with and will best meet the needs of the group. An *outreach* Bible study group would not usually use material such as grief recovery, parenting, church history, etc. How-ever, groups using these and other materials can be outreach oriented. That is, following the completion of the particular topic, the group leader can suggest that the members join a Bible study group. The Bible study group may begin as a nurture/study group. Later the individual can be invited to attend a group study that is more doctrinal/decision oriented.

Because not every individual is ready for a doctrinal/decision-oriented Bible study group, I am going to suggest two tracks that may be followed.

I. *Needs-oriented Track*

Step 1: Grief Recovery Group (other felt need topics can be studied).

Upon completion the group leader invites the participants to join a nonthreatening Bible study group.

Step 2: Nurture/Bible Study Group

The emphasis is upon understanding how the Bible can meet the needs of everyday life. The group is introduced to Jesus, the plan of salvation, and Christ's life on this earth. A study in the

Gospels is very appropriate for this level. As you're studying together, certain doctrines will naturally emerge from the Scripture and be discussed. However, this is not the time or place to give a full Bible study on a topic unless the group requests it or an individual has an interest.

Step 3: Doctrinal Bible Study Group

Once the group has completed Step 2, the group leader states something like this. "As we have studied John's Gospel on the life of Christ, various subjects have arisen, such as heaven, salvation, and the coming of Jesus. I thought it would be good for our group to study these topics together. If you are interested, tell me, and in a few weeks, when this study ends, we will have a topical study."

Step 4: Further Study

This would include a group baptismal class, individual lessons, and continued group studies. The details will be discussed later in the chapter on follow-up.

II. *Bible Study-oriented Track*

Step 1: Book of the Bible

Choose for your study a book of the Bible with which the leader is comfortable and interested. Invite individuals to attend. Interest will arise as various teachings and doctrinal points surface in the chapter-by-chapter study.

Step 2: Doctrinal Bible Study Group

Once the group has completed Step 2, the group leader states something like this. "As we have studied Mark's Gospel together on the life of Christ, various subjects have arisen such as heaven, salvation, and the coming of Jesus. I thought it would be good for our group to study these topics together. If you are interested, tell me, and in a few weeks, when this study ends, we will have a topical study."

Step 3: Further Study

This would include a group baptismal class, individual lessons, and continued group studies. The details will be discussed later in the chapter on follow-up.

Study Material Selection

Materials available on the market for small group Bible studies are numerous. However, Seventh-day Adventist Bible studies designed specifically for small groups are just emerging. Once an individual understands the principles of small groups and the dynamics that take place, they can adapt some lessons designed for the classroom setting to the small group setting.

CHAPTER

8

Obtaining Group Members

As one begins to establish a study group, there are several methods that may be utilized with proven success. This chapter will consider several ways of obtaining group members and how to be successful in growing a group.

One important lesson learned in studying groups, is that it is a mistake to rely upon the handbill as the primary advertising. In fact, a handbill should not even be considered a key part of an advertising program. The handbill should be viewed as a bonus item. The key to a successful small group is a personal invitation to those with whom you are acquainted. Experience reveals that there are very few individuals who will attend a home setting because of a handbill. Most people feel comfortable going to a church or public building to attend a seminar. But to go to a private home where there may be several people they do not know is difficult for them.

Because many hesitate to respond to our familiar handbill method, it is imperative to encourage and inform church members that the success of small group outreach will depend upon the personal invitations they make.

Personal Invitation

Consider inviting these individuals to your group:

1. Neighbors.
2. Friends.
3. Work associates.
4. Relatives.

5. Others, such as service station attendant, hairdresser, banker, grocery store clerk, etc.

Experience has revealed that as people in a neighborhood are invited, the individuals who live near the visitor, but have never met him or her before, are unlikely to attend. However, if in walking around the block the visitor has spoken to someone and simply said "Hello," or "Your flowers are pretty," etc.—these individuals are more open to attending than if they had never before met their neighbor. This program's strength depends upon previously established relationships.

This was illustrated graphically by George. He was sitting in my office frustrated. He had visited more than 30 homes in his neighborhood and invited his neighbors to attend. The first night not one neighbor attended. Further questioning revealed that George wasn't acquainted with his neighbors. Even though he had lived in his neighborhood for two years, his busy schedule kept him from becoming known to his neighbors.

As an individual begins to organize a small group in his home, the SDA members who will be attending should make a list of their own acquaintances and begin to invite them. The neighbors living around the host home should receive an invitation. It is best for the owners of the home to invite their neighbors. However, the group leader and the homeowners can visit and invite the neighbors together.

Those who visit should take an invitation with them. The same invitation can be used by other group members as they invite their acquaintances.

Sample Invitation
(inside only)

You're invited to a Bible study in our home. We'll be studying the book of Revelation. This is the last book in the Bible, and it has a special message for us today. We hope that you will join us.

Our Address: _____

Day: _____

Time: _____

Phone: _____

A Suggested Approach in Giving a Personal Invitation

As you approach your neighbor, say something similar to this: "Hello, John. How are you today?"

"Fine, Kurt. Thank you."

"John, in three weeks I am going to have an informal Bible study group in my home. I am inviting my friends and neighbors to come and study the book of Revelation together (or other books of the Bible that you are studying). I don't know if you have ever studied the book of Revelation or not. I have found it to be intriguing and helpful in understanding the perplexing times in which we live. The study is informal and designed for those who are beginners or old-timers when it comes to Bible study. If you decide to come, please give me a call."

Telephone Invitation

The next-best thing to a personal invitation is a telephone invitation. When calling, rather than visiting friends or neighbors, use a conversation similar to the one above. Follow up conversations by sending personal invitations or hand-delivering them as outlined above.

Mailing personal invitation cards or follow-up visits are vital to the success of telephone invitations. The reason for this is that the individual can hold something in his hand that reminds him of the meeting. Also, the extra effort reveals your genuine desire for him to attend. Experience indicates a higher *success* rate if you follow both steps.

Yard Signs

The yard sign is a poster that states "Neighborhood Home Bible Study Group." The sign resembles a "FOR SALE" sign in size and quality. The sign is to be placed in the yard of the host home. The purpose of the sign is twofold. Individuals who are coming to a small group meeting can use the sign as an assistance in locating the home. Also, the sign can cause interest to arise in the minds of the neighbors.

Experience has shown that some people are hesitant about placing the sign in their front yards. If this is the case, then encourage the host to place the sign in his front yard near the beginning date and for the first several meetings as a location sign.

Sample Yard Sign

```
NEIGHBORHOOD HOME BIBLE STUDY
        on the book of Revelation
             Day: Tuesday
            Time: 7:00 p.m.
          YOU are welcome!
```

Welcome Poster

This poster is to be used on or near your front door. The purpose is to identify your home as the correct location, and to extend to the group members the thought that you are happy to have them come.

Sample Welcome Poster

```
WELCOME
to our
Home Bible Study
```

Handbill

A specially prepared handbill can be mailed on a mass basis if your church desires to conduct a number of small groups simultaneously. If this is the case, you need to determine the approximate number of individuals you expect to respond and prepare accordingly.

Reminder: Don't rely upon the handbill for your main advertising. Remember, the handbill is simply a bonus methodology. Very few people respond to a handbill for a home Bible study group.

Handbill Methodology

A central phone number should be provided on the handbill. As persons call the number they should be directed to the group nearest their home. The caller should receive a letter with details concerning the small group plus a visit or call from the group leader. The following is a sample phone response and letter.

Phone Response

"Hello, you have reached Neighborhood Home Bible Studies. May I help you?"

"Yes, I would like to register to attend a study group."

"Good! I'm glad you called. I'll take some information over the phone, and we will get you registered. I need your name, address, and phone number."

Step 1: Assignment to Study Group

As soon as possible, determine which study group, having

available space, the individual is closest to and contact them with the information. After you have contacted the individual, write a letter of welcome similar to the one below. The letter should be signed by the group leader.

Step 2: Sample Confirmation Letter

Betty Jones
10 NE. 82nd Avenue
Anytown, U.S.A. 12345
Dear Mrs. Jones:

I am happy that you will be a member of the study group meeting at Fred and Linda Smith's home. The address is 1603 N.E. 196th Avenue. Our first meeting is Monday evening, February 5, at 7:00. My name is Kurt Johnson. I will be the group leader.

I have found the book of Revelation to be an interesting and intriguing book. God has given a message in Revelation that assists each of us in practical daily living. As our group studies together, not only will the study be enriching, but the sharing of ideas and friendship will be enjoyable. There will be 8 to 12 persons in our study group.

I am looking forward to your being a part of our group. If you have any questions, please give me a call at 483-1020. Fred and Linda's phone number is 481-6731.

Sincerely,
Kurt Johnson

Step 3: Confirmation Visit

After the letter has been mailed, it would be good to wait a few days and then stop by for a brief visit. The visit should only be about five minutes long, and will probably be done on the front porch.

As the leader visits, he or she should take an invitation or card along with the name, address, and phone number of the host/hostess, the leader's name and phone number, and the day of the week plus the time and date of the first meeting.

The introductory conversation would be similar to this:

"Hello, are you Betty Jones?"

"Yes."

"Mrs. Jones, I am Kurt Johnson. Last week you registered for a home Bible study group on the book of Revelation. I sent you a letter the first of the week concerning the details, which I hope you have received. I wanted to take a moment to stop by and introduce myself before our group meets next Monday."

"It is nice to meet you Mr. Johnson. Would you like to come in?" (You could go in if you desired; however, you want the visit to be brief. I would suggest the following reply.)

"I appreciate the invitation: however, I have several visits to make tonight. Maybe some other time we can talk more. I'm really happy you will be part of our group. Here's a card with the details on it. Do you have any questions?"

"Not at the moment. I'm looking forward to coming. I'm a little nervous, but excited."

"I understand how you feel, but just relax. Soon you'll know those in the group. Before you know it, we'll all be friends. I'll see you Monday. It was nice meeting you."

Don't overlook any of the steps. It's a temptation to simply receive the telephone call and mail the confirmation letter while overlooking the visit. Experience has revealed that because the registrants are attending a home rather than a public building, all steps are needed for success!

Step 4: Visiting Non-attenders

Following your first study group, those who registered and didn't attend should be visited or receive a phone call. The contact should be brief. Simply tell the person you missed them. Convey to him or her that the group study went well and was a learning experience with a relaxed atmosphere. Tell the individual you hope he can attend next Monday evening.

Techniques for Growing Your Existing Group and Starting New Groups

One goal of a small group is to expand the benefits of small group ministry to others. The purpose of this expansion to others is outreach (lead them to accept Jesus), and nurture (assist in their Christian development).

Every small group needs to have evangelism as its emphasis, otherwise it can become a clique or closed society, and visitors will be viewed as intruders. Here are several ways to begin new groups:

1. Empty-Chair Principle. Each group should have an empty chair in its circle at each meeting. The chair should be filled at the next meeting as group members invite other persons to attend. Your group should pray each week for God to lead someone to the next meeting. As the group grows by this process it will eventually divide to form a new group.

2. Sometimes existing group members, or others who desire to belong to a study group, cannot attend the existing group because of scheduling or location conflicts. To assist with this difficulty a new group should be started.

3. Invite individuals from:
   a. church interest lists
   b. newly baptized members
   c. visitors to church
   d. former members
   e. friends, work associates
   f. others

4. Conduct a revival or evangelistic meeting, and invite those attending to form small group Bible studies.

5. Whenever you have one person who desires to study the Bible, form a small group and invite others.

Remember, two people can begin a small group! Being small is not a reason to not begin. The Holy Spirit and personal invitations will grow your group.

There are several steps that Garrie Williams and Kurt

Johnson in Oregon have discovered are successful for a pastor and lay member to begin small group ministries in the local church. These items are as follows:

How a Church Pastor Can Begin a Small Group Ministry

• Through study and prayer, become familiar with all aspects of small group outreach and nurture ministry. If possible, attend a small group seminar.

• Preach sermons on how small group ministries are avenues for the Holy Spirit to meet the felt needs of individuals.

• Choose a group of potential small group leaders and begin meeting weekly with them. Teach them to be small group leaders by instructing and modeling how to lead a small group. Provide them with books on small group ministries.

• Organize a small group leadership training weekend and invite all interested church members to attend. Following the weekend, many of them can join groups with trained leaders. Members may then desire training to become small group leaders.

• Continue to have weekly leaders' meetings conducted and/or supported by the pastor.

• As groups begin, incorporate experiences and prayer requests into the Sabbath morning services. As group participants share, this will inspire others to join a group.

• Include in the church bulletin and newsletters information concerning times, dates, and locations of the groups.

• Have a special consecration service on Sabbath morning for new group leaders—asking the congregation to remember them in prayer.

• Not all church members will be comfortable in small groups, so continue a prayer meeting, Daniel and Revelation seminars, health ministry activities, and other outreach methodologies.

• Plan on regular baptismal classes, evangelistic meetings,

Bible studies, pastor's class, and other activities to aid in reaping those who make decisions for Jesus and the church.

How a Lay Member Can Begin a Small Group Ministry

• Prayerfully study information on starting and leading groups. Pray earnestly for the leading of the Holy Spirit in seeking God's wisdom and guidance.

• Make an appointment with your pastor. Express your desire to begin a small group ministry in your home. Ask your pastor for counsel, help, and prayer.

• If possible, attend a small group training seminar.

• Select a fellow church member to be your assistant leader. Meet together regularly, asking God for guidance as you plan your small group.

• If the leader or assistant leader is not using their home for the group meeting place, ask a friend if you can use their home.

• Make a prospect list, including individuals in your neighborhood, and invite them to your group.

• The leader and assistant leader should request a weekly or bi-weekly meeting with their pastor. At this meeting discuss the study material, share experiences, ask questions, request assistance with receiving decisions, baptismal classes, reaping meetings, and other areas of concern.

• As opportunities arise, share group experiences with members on Sabbath morning.

• Recruit and train potential small group leaders, incorporating them into the regular meeting with the pastor.

CHAPTER
9

Opening Night

I remember sitting in a seminary preaching class, listening to fellow pastors share their personal feelings about preaching Sabbath sermons. The discussion centered around having a nervous stomach, tension, and what is called "the preacher's edge."

Everyone who is a public speaker, whether he is a television personality, an evangelist, Revelation Seminar instructor, or a Sabbath school teacher, has experienced tension and apprehension.

As a leader, you probably will not be able to escape some of those feelings on the first night of your group. However, you have a distinct advantage. You are a child of God—called to speak for Jesus. Those who are called are also empowered. Those who are empowered discover that Jesus melts tension and apprehension, and with the disappearance of tension comes the power and words from God that will enable your group to become acquainted with Jesus.

On the first night, have those assisting with the group meet about 45 minutes before starting time. Once the room is prepared, and the final preparations are made, have a season of prayer together. The basic preparation would include:

- Turning on the outside house lights.
- Arranging extra chairs in the meeting room.
- Having extra Bibles on hand.
- Having the first night's study guides available.

Once everyone has arrived, there are several things the

leader will take care of the first night that will not be necessary on succeeding study nights.

1. Introduce the group members.

Remember that some of your members will be somewhat apprehensive. Do not do anything to embarrass them. Do not ask them which church they attend. Do not ask too many details about their personal lives (such as work, family, etc.) unless it comes up naturally in the conversation. There will be many study nights together in which this information can be shared. If a person is a stranger, say something similar to this as you introduce him or her. "This is Brenda Jensen. We met for the first time tonight. I am really happy she came, and I am looking forward to becoming better acquainted with her." If the leader is introducing a friend, he may say, "this is Fred Thomas. Fred works with me at Pacific Power and Light Company."

2. Share basic group guidelines.

Following the introductions, the leader should share some information to assist the group members in relaxing. An example would be: "Now that we know each other's names, it won't be long before our name tags will be unnecessary. I want to share some items with each of you to help you understand the basics of our group study. First, we are here as a group to be friends. Each person is important. As we study together, our viewpoints may differ. This is to be expected as we are all different people with different backgrounds. Some of us may never have studied the Bible before. Others may be well acquainted with the Scriptures. Whatever your background, it is OK! All of us had to begin sometime. No matter how much Bible study you have done, your viewpoint is important.

"No one will ever be asked or expected to read, pray, or give an opinion unless it is your choice. Experience has shown, if we are a typical group, and I'm sure we are, that some of us like to speak and participate more than others. It's my intention that you'll never be made to feel uncomfortable.

If you have trouble finding a Bible verse, don't be too embarrassed to ask for help. There was a time in my life when I had to ask for someone to assist me.

"When I invited you to come, I shared with you that our study would be on the book of Revelation [or whatever topic you are studying], and that the purpose would be for Bible study, sharing, and becoming better acquainted with one another. The details we will work out together in a few minutes. If at any time you're uncomfortable about anything, please tell me.

"I want to share Judy's [group hostess] responsibilities with you. Judy, as you might have guessed by now, is our hostess. This is her home. I'm glad she's letting us meet here. If the telephone rings, or someone knocks on the door, Judy will answer the door or phone for us. If during the meeting you need something, Judy will help you. Just get up quietly and ask her.

"While we are giving details, the bathroom is down the hallway on the left. Feel free to get up during our meeting and use the bathroom if needed. There are drinking glasses in the kitchen, and a telephone. Judy will assist you if you need a drink or want to use the phone."

3. The group covenant/contract.

After the group guidelines have been explained, the leader should pass out the first lesson if it has the group covenant included in it. If the lesson does not have the group covenant printed, then print the covenant on a separate sheet and give it to the members. The following is a typical group covenant.

Group Covenant

Purpose of our group:

_____

_____

We will meet as follows:
Days of the week _____

Beginning time _____

Closing time _____

Meeting place _____

Typical schedule for Bible study:

_____

_____

Individual preparation: _____

_____

Group leaders: _____

_____

Host/Hostess: _____

_____

The leader will guide the group through the covenant. The covenant is simply the agreement the group members make together about how the group will function.

The group covenant is an extremely important part of the small group Bible study. Experience has shown that if a covenant is not used, the group will have a tendency to lose cohesiveness.

A group covenant:
> Defines group members' expectations.
> Provides accountability to one another.
> Enhances commitment to the group.
> Provides a basis by which to evaluate your group's success ratio.
> Establishes the purpose of the group.

Some of the areas to consider under each section would be as follows:

Purpose of Our Group

Ask the members about their expectations. What do they want to happen? The types of answers the leader desires to receive are Bible study, prayer, sharing, and fellowship.

We Will Meet as Follows
The group needs to agree upon the day of the week they will meet, and the length of the meeting. A typical length is one and a half to two hours. The beginning and starting time should also be agreed upon. In most cases the meeting place has been predetermined. Share with the members the number of weeks needed to complete the study guides. If a group member has scheduling conflicts with the determined group meeting schedule, try to arrange for him or her to meet with another group, or if possible, start another group!

Typical Schedule for Bible Study
Ask the group how much time they want to spend on each item every night. The items are sharing, Bible study, and prayer. A typical amount for an hour and a half meeting would be: sharing—15 minutes; Bible study—60 minutes; prayer time—15 minutes. It is the group leader's responsibility to keep things on schedule. Experience has shown that as the group members become better acquainted, it grows harder to stay on schedule. Remember that some members may have to get up early for work the next morning. If you go past the scheduled time, they may drop out of the group.

Individual Preparation
Let them know that each week, when the study ends, members will be given the next week's lesson to take home. It's best if they can read through it and fill out as much as possible before the next meeting.

Group Leaders
Have the group members write down the leader's name

and phone number for future reference.

Host/Hostess

Have the group members write down the host's/hostess's name and phone number for future reference.

4. Introduce the Bible.

Because some may not be acquainted with Scripture, explain some of the basics. Don't ask if anyone needs an introduction, just assume someone does. Show the book list in the front of the Bible, including the page numbers to locate each book. Explain about the Old and New Testaments. Demonstrate how to locate a book, chapter, and verse.

5. Introduce the study guides.

Give each member the first study guide. Explain to them the three basic sections of each lesson. These are the sharing, or getting acquainted, section; the Bible study; and the personal response section.

Do only a small portion of the study guide the first night in order for the group members to understand the format you will follow. Then have the members take the lesson home and bring it back the next week for discussion and study.

6. Prayer Time.

For many, the prayer time will cause apprehension if they think they may have to pray. For the first several weeks, the leader or assistant should give the closing prayer after the members have had an opportunity to present prayer requests. When the leader believes the time is appropriate, the group members may be taught how to pray together as a group. Always remind the group members that not everyone is expected to pray.

Important! Never go around the circle during prayer time, sharing time, or Bible study for participation. Always let the members speak spontaneously.

Second Group Meeting

During the second meeting, take time to introduce new members and to refresh the members' memories of the other participants' names. Remind the group of the agreed-upon time commitments and proceed with the meeting. Remember at the end of each meeting to give the group members the next study guide.

To assist you in understanding a typical small group study guide, a sample has been included (see Appendix).

Conversational Prayer

Some time following the initial group meeting, the leader should introduce the concept of conversational prayer. This section will assist in this process.

Does public prayer make you nervous? If your answer is yes, then you are not alone. Many Christians experience nervous feelings when they pray aloud. They are afraid of sounding foolish, of not knowing what to say, or of being judged by others. Fear of prayer will disappear as a group learns the basics of praying together. Tell your group members that no one will be pressured to pray. If they want to pray, they can, at their own speed. The key is to speak to God with openness of heart.

There are several guidelines to follow to teach your group to pray together.

1. As a leader, model how to pray by praying first. After the leader prays, others will continue.

2. Don't spend too much time sharing prayer requests. Pray for the needs of the group. If another group member wishes to pray for the same item or need, he may, or simply say amen as the individual concludes his prayer.

3. Select one topic at a time as your group is learning to pray together. Some groups have a three-pronged prayer. First, the members begin by praising and thanking God in prayer. Second, the members pray about needs outside the group (friends, events, situations, etc.). Third, the group prays

71

for needs within the group (family, self, fellow group members, the group, etc.).

4. The group should next pray for the "empty chair" to be filled by a new group member.

5. The group can conclude by saying the Lord's Prayer together. Saying the prayer together gives every group member an opportunity to pray. Many members will not know the Lord's Prayer. Copies should be made available for each member.

CHAPTER
10

Visitation and Obtaining Decisions

The methods of visitation and receiving decisions in a small group setting are much different from the approach that is taken in an evangelistic meeting or Revelation Seminar conducted in a public building. Most of us who have become accustomed to the methodologies utilized in previous evangelistic approaches need time for education and discussion of the approach in small groups. It is essential for the pastor to spend time discussing visitation and decision-making techniques with his group leaders and participating church members. If this is not done, the members may become frustrated with the lack of decisions made in the small group settings. Also, SDA group members may become frustrated with the interaction process if they do not understand the small group evangelistic method.

In an evangelistic series or Revelation Seminar, utilizing a teacher-listener approach, the decision making process involves marking a card or box on a lesson. The teacher can read the responses and then visit the individuals to discuss their decision. In the small group there is continual feedback. Persons are able to share opinions and discuss negative and positive responses to a specific question or Scripture. Because of this, you have interaction taking place every moment throughout the study group. In most cases you will know immediately what the individual is thinking and how he or she is relating to a particular subject or question. Because of this, the approach needs to be different from a classroom setting.

As Christians we are anxious for others to accept Jesus as their Saviour, to accept the biblical teachings of the Seventh-day Adventist Church, and to begin to attend our church services. It is easy for us as Seventh-day Adventist Christians to be zealous, and to feel that at every opportunity we should mention our religious beliefs. We need to remember that in a small group setting we do not need to voice our opinion at every occasion. As long as a person is attending the group, opportunities will continue to exist. The group members' current spiritual growth must be kept in mind as we determine how much to say or not say. The individual's presence in the meeting allows the Holy Spirit to work upon his heart and mind.

The group leader should always desire and look for situations in which he can invite an individual to attend church, to make a decision for Christ, or to become a Seventh-day Adventist. However, invitations should be given at appropriate times and in the proper settings.

In the small group setting the most appropriate situation for receiving decision commitments is on a private one-to-one basis, and not in the group. When an individual is approached while the group is in process, it can be embarrassing for the individual and for other group members. It is appropriate in the group setting to give your personal testimony about what Christ means to you, how special your church is to you, or extend an invitation to attend church or another meeting. Wisdom and discretion, however, are necessary.

The group members need to be talked to in regard to their utilization of SDA terminology and how they talk about other denominations and members of other churches. A negative statement made in sincerity, and in some cases truthfully, may not be understood by someone else of a different denomination or spiritual maturity in Christ. We must always speak judiciously and wisely.

As indicated earlier, the study guides and the atmosphere

in the study group are informal and relaxed. The desire is that decisions will be made, and that they will be encouraged in a nonpressured setting. Every study guide utilizes decision-making questions to be answered privately, yet with a voluntary opportunity to be vocalized.

As a group leader, be alert to those who have made decisions, those struggling with conscience, and those responding passively. As the group members grow in their discovery of biblical knowledge, the group leader should respond to them as follows:

1. Affirm them during and/or after the study. Say things like, "John, I am happy you accepted Jesus as your Saviour," or, "John, I want you to know I appreciate you sharing your struggle. I will do whatever I can to assist you."

2. After the study (or before it begins) make a point of talking to a group member who has made a decision or is struggling with a decision. Begin the conversation this way: "Mary, tonight you indicated that it was a shock to you to discover that Saturday is the day of worship. You seemed troubled. Would you like to spend some time this week talking about it?" If Mary's response is positive, arrange a time at her house or yours. If her response is negative, then simply say "If you ever want to talk, let me know" or "I have some booklets on the subject you might enjoy reading."

3. If the group leader ever feels that a private conversation with a group member concerning his response to the group, biblical material, etc., is needed, stop by for a visit or make a phone call.

4. As group members grow and respond, a note of encouragement mailed to them from the group leader would be appropriate.

5. An invitation to lunch at the leader's house or a restaurant, a shopping trip, or a picnic offers an appropriate method of becoming closer to a group member and gaining opportunities for discussion.

6. The group leader should always be alert for the oppor-

tunity to share his personal testimony with a group member privately or to lead him in making a decision for Jesus Christ.

7. The SDA group members should be reminded that as they discuss their own local church experiences and activities in the group, it should be done in a positive manner. Negative comments concerning a person or program have no place in a small group setting. It is helpful, however, in appropriate situations to make positive comments about your church or a member. This plants a seed of interest in the minds of group members.

8. It is important that the SDA group members remember that the goal is to become friends with non-Adventist group members and assist them in growing in the knowledge of the Lord. Because someone has a belief, an attitude, or a response that is not as others believe, does not mean that the others have to combat the opinion. The group leader's goal is to accept each as a person, to pray for them as they continue to attend, and at the appropriate time assist them, by the use of Scripture coupled with the power of the Holy Spirit, in changing their particular viewpoint. An example would be someone mentioning that he enjoys the use of alcoholic beverages. Our place is not to condemn him, but to accept the fact that this is where he is at this *moment* in his spiritual growth.

At the appropriate time, by the power of the Holy Spirit and the grace of God, we will assist him in overcoming his negative habit.

I'm reminded again of Ellen White's statement in *Evangelism*, p. 12: "You need not feel that all the truth is to be spoken to unbelievers on any and every occasion. You should plan carefully what to say and what to leave unsaid. This is not practicing deception; it is to work as Paul worked."

Wisdom and tact are a vital part of small group evangelism! God will provide this as we seek Him for guidance. Visiting a group member in his home, or talking to him after the meeting regarding commitment or the Scriptures, is always appropriate. The key ingredients to decision-making in small groups are first to look for responsive signs in word or action in your group, and then visit them in their home.

Four Steps in Small Group Evangelistic Planning

There are four organizational steps that, if followed, will successfully bring a small group member into active Seventh-day Adventist Church membership.

Step 1 is getting people to attend the initial group meeting. The purpose of attending the initial meeting is to acquaint them with the Scriptures, with Jesus Christ, and with the Seventh-day Adventist Church.

Approximately three to four weeks before the group completes the study guides, the leader should mention to the group that for those who desire, the leader will continue the group.

Once the leader announces the prospect of the group continuing, Step 2 should be taken. In this step the group leader evaluates each member to determine what type of classes would be best for him if he chooses not to continue with the group. In some cases the person might continue with the group but may not be ready for advanced studies. Following the evaluation, the leader should visit each member individually in their homes or after the group meeting, and determine further studies for each individual.

Some of the options available should be:

1. Continued group study utilizing lessons on a book of the Bible
2. Continued in-depth study of one subject
3. Group member begins study group in his own home
4. Group baptismal/doctrinal class
5. Individual Bible studies in the home
6. Sabbath school class
7. Pastor's Bible class on Sabbath mornings

8. No further studies. Continue to visit periodically for continued friendship.

One of the vital roles of the small group is the benefit it provides for nurturing the individual. If a person chooses individual assistance, try to involve him eventually in a small group process.

Other factors that are excellent bridges from the small group to the Sabbath school are:

1. The small group leader is a Sabbath school teacher and invites the members to their small group at Sabbath school.

2. The small group leader or other SDA group members invite the non-SDA small group members to the small group (Sabbath school class) they belong to at church.

3. The small group leader introduces the group member to their pastor. Once there is an acquaintance, the group member who is interested in the SDA Church is invited to become a part of the pastor's class.

As you invite the group members to Sabbath school, sit with them and introduce them to other church members.

Experience has shown that Step 3 is essential to receive the maximum number of decisions from a small group. Step 3 is a series of decision/reaping meetings. The meetings can be anywhere from a two-week series to a traditional four- to six-week evangelistic series. A two-week series conducted by the local church pastor using altar calls or decision cards is very effective. When the pastor does the speaking in these decision meetings, it is a natural connection to the local church for the group member.

The small group leader needs to invite the group members to attend the meetings. Offer to pick up members. Have the group meet at the church and sit together.

Step 4 is critical to the assimilation of the individual into the church. Once the group member has made a decision to attend church, join the pastor's class, or a baptismal class, an SDA group member should attend with him. The member should sit with him, answer questions, model Sabbath-keeping, and assist with the person's complete discipling process.

11

Questions Commonly Asked

There are numerous questions that arise concerning groups not only from beginners, but seasoned pros. This section will deal with the questions most frequently asked.

I. I don't want anyone smoking in my house, but one of the group members smokes. What should I do?

There are several successful approaches to take in this situation. The easiest is to have a five-minute break just prior to the Bible study time. This allows for no interruptions during the study. One or two individuals can accompany the smokers outside and chat with them while they are smoking.

The second approach is to have an understanding that if someone can't wait to smoke during the group meeting, he should get up and go out on the porch and then return. The problem with this approach is that it focuses attention on the individual and may embarrass him so he won't return. Also, they might have to leave at a vital part of the discussion.

II. Is it necessary to serve food at each meeting?

Some small group instructors say that food is an important ingredient of every meeting because it is an excellent social icebreaker. However, experience has shown that small groups can be very successful without food.

In fact, serving food has its negative side. Weekly preparation becomes a chore, and not everyone will be able to supply the same quality of food each week. The risk is always there to hurt a group member's feelings if food is brought that others might choose not to eat because of health or religious convictions.

It is appropriate, however, to occasionally have a soup, salad, and bread potluck or a treat if it is a group member's birthday or another special event.

III. Should an offering be taken in a home group meeting?

The answer is no. It is very inexpensive to conduct a home meeting. Study guides for six to eight members will be only a few dollars. It is very awkward to ask for an offering from six people whom you have invited to your home. However, some groups ask the members to purchase their own materials. This has worked with success. If finances are a difficulty, ask your local church for assistance. Almost every church has a budget for Bible study material.

IV. What is the pastor's role in small groups in the local church?

The pastor's leadership and support in the small group organizational and functioning process is the difference between success and mediocrity. While it is true that small group leadership and participation is a lay member's responsibility, pastor involvement is *vitally necessary*.

The pastor should provide the following leadership ingredients:

1. Publicly share with his church members his personal convictions concerning the importance of small groups.

2. Preach a sermon or sermons on the biblical basis and necessity for small group meetings.

3. Provide time each Sabbath in church for the members to share their group experiences. This will inspire others to desire to become involved.

4. The pastor should meet regularly with his small group leaders. At this meeting he should:

    a.) pray with and for his group leaders

b.) answer questions

c.) allow the leaders to share their positive and negative experiences

d.) provide a brief outline of the next week's study guide if all groups are using the same material

e.) discuss the lesson and answer questions to assist the group leaders

f.) provide resources for the teachers to use in preparing their biblical material

5. Keep accurate up-to-date records concerning the spiritual development of the members attending the groups.

6. Assist the lay leader in visitation and development of follow-up classes and groups for the group members.

7. Provide continual training in small groups and evangelism techniques for his lay leaders.

Again, the pastor's support and involvement in small group ministry is the difference between success and mediocrity in the church's group program.

V. Is it possible to modify small group study guide materials to be used in a classroom style of teaching?

Although small group study material is designed to be used in the small group home setting, some have utilized the material in a classroom environment with success. If you find yourself in a situation best served by a classroom style, but want to apply small group material, provide a room in which individuals can sit around tables, or place their chairs in a circle or, sit in sections of the sanctuary in pews, but clustered together.

The leader would guide the entire teaching process from the front of the room. An introduction to the lesson would be given by the leader. Following the introduction, the leader would have the members share the interaction questions in their small group. If the class members are not in clusters, then the leader can ask for volunteers in the group to share with the entire group.

A better way, however, would be for the class members to share with the person sitting next to them. The leader would then guide the Bible study with the entire group. Periodically, the leader could have the class members share with the person sitting next to them, or if the class is in clusters, the members can share among themselves, or the sharing can come from volunteers within the entire group.

Because the study guide is used in a large group, the leader may not know how the group members are responding individually to the subject matter. Also, the leader will have no way to hear or respond to the discussion concerning a person's response to accepting Jesus or a particular doctrine. Consequently, an organized visitation program to determine the interest of the individuals is essential.

During the visit, answer questions and offer reading material dealing with subjects of interest. At the meeting, decision cards may be used.

If the classroom method is utilized, remember to provide a warm, nonthreatening atmosphere. If this is not done, your attendance will usually decrease.

VI. What are a few of the basic small group principles that are essential for a successful small group ministry?

There are numerous principles that could be considered. In fact, entire books have been written on the subject. Larry R. Evans, author of two booklets on small groups, discusses numerous principles that are basic to any group. Following are some key characteristics I've observed:

1. There is no substitute for the presence of the Holy Spirit. All the theory, planning, energy, effort, and good intentions will be to no avail if God is not put first in the personal life of the leader. It is essential for the leader to provide personal time for his or her own spiritual growth and to ensure that Jesus is the focus of the group's activities.

2. The seating arrangement in a small group fellowship is best in a circle, so all can see and participate. Rows of chairs

are appropriate for a class, but not a study group.

3. Unconditional love and acceptance are prerequisites for a successful small group.

4. Conflict and tension may arise in your small group. An atmosphere of trust and acceptance from the very beginning will assist with this dilemma.

5. Positive interaction between group members is essential. The group leader will need to be alert to dealing with the talkative and silent members.

6. A small group goes through "four seasons of development." These are honeymoon, disillusionment, synthesis, and culmination. The group leader needs to be aware of each and prepare for them.

7. Competitive/defensive attitudes can arise between two or more group members. This can be destructive to the success of your group.

8. There are five levels of verbal communication that your group members will possess. In order for the group members to internalize the facts of Scripture, they must individually experience these levels. The levels are cliché, conversation, reporting facts/ideas/judgments, feelings and emotions, openness, and personal commitment.

9. The group leader sets the tone and climate for the small group. The leader must be empathic, warm, genuine, and alert to possible group problems.

10. Affirmation of each group member is essential to the personal and spiritual growth of the individuals. Stating or demonstrating that you see and appreciate various qualities they possess will strengthen the member and the group.

11. Developing and maintaining trust within the group is essential to an effective group. Trust is developed by time, experience, and a demonstration of acceptance and support.

12. In addition to learning biblical knowledge, individuals need to talk about the impact of the material on their personal life (past, present, and future).

13. Negative behavior can occur in a group because of

home difficulties, work pressures, reactions to Bible study material, an adverse relationship with a group member, etc. Redemptive fellowship will provide an atmosphere in which these feelings can be aired.

14. As group members become disenchanted with some aspect of the group's dynamics they will consider dropping out. There will be "cries of help" before they quit. The process is usually threefold. The person gives an excuse for possibly quitting, misses a meeting, and then drops out completely. Be alert for cries of help.

15. When the group progresses in its biblical study, you as leader will desire to see change in the lives of your group members. If it does not occur, remember to still love and accept them. Change is encouraged but not required.

16. Prayer is the key to power in our small group. Remember to pray daily for each member and group meeting.

17. As group members become exposed to biblical knowledge, some will be convicted to make decisions on the knowledge gained. Be alert to a group member's receptiveness and provide the opportunity for specific decisions.

18. Your group will eventually arrive at the date of its agreed length of time to meet. When this occurs, try making arrangements to continue meeting the needs of the group members. This is a pastoral responsibility of your leadership.

VII. Are there unique points to be aware of on a school campus in conducting small groups?

A campus provides an ideal setting for a small group ministry. Consider the following points: Many student groups meet for one hour per week rather than one and a half to two hours because of busy schedules. Some groups prefer to be open to new members for only 4 to 6 weeks or less. The group may choose an outreach project. Most student groups plan to meet for the school year and then recontract quarterly as work and study schedules change. Small groups on campus have

been successful as nurture and outreach tools for students'
spiritual growth.

CHAPTER
12

God Honors Vision

The book of Proverbs states: "Where there is no vision, the people perish" (Prov. 29:18). Vision is as necessary today as it was then.

• Adam and Eve possessed vision when they looked for a son to be the Redeemer.

• Abraham had vision when God promised that he would be father to a nation more numerous than the stars in heaven.

• Hosea had a vision of hope when he brought back his wife, Gomer.

• Zerubbabel had a vision when he led the Israelites to rebuild Jerusalem.

• Mary had a vision when she accepted the responsibility of being the mother of Jesus.

• Lydia, Priscilla, and Aquila had a vision when they opened up their homes to church fellowship groups.

One of the fundamental points of the Christian faith is that God honors vision! God desires His people to see beyond the obstacles of life to the prospects of what He can do through a dedicated, committed, trusting people.

Is it possible for you to lead a home study group?

Is it possible for you to open your home for a study group?

Is it possible for hundreds and thousands of homes to be opened for Bible study throughout your conference, the division, the world?

Through faith, the power of the Holy Spirit, claiming the promises of God, and stepping out in active faith, all things are possible!

Paul said: "I can do all things through Christ who strengthens me" (Phil. 4:13, NKJV).

Jesus said in Matthew 17:20: ". . . if you have faith as a mustard seed, you will say to this mountain, 'Move from here to there,' and it will move; and nothing will be impossible for you" (NKJV).

Referring to the days in which we live, Ellen White wrote of the need for companies of church members going from door to door opening the Bible to their neighbors.

Why not bow your head in prayer right now and ask God to reveal how you can be a part of His vision for His remnant people?

NEIGHBORHOOD HOME BIBLE STUDY®
A Window To John's Gospel

Introduction to John 2

Chapter two opens with two of Jesus' "firsts:" His first "sign," turning water into wine at the wedding in Cana (2:1-11), and His first confrontation, in the temple (2:12-25).

It is important to understand that Jesus' first sign was not simply a miracle. Rather, the Beloved Disciple presents the sign as an acted-out symbol of Jesus' Passion (suffering, death, and resurrection); references to Jesus' "time" (verse 4) usually refer to His Passion (7:6, 8, 30; 8:20; 12:23, 27; 13:1; 17:1). Jesus' sign builds His disciples' faith, yet Mary's misunderstanding ultimately evaporates only at Jesus' crucifixion — Christ's "highpoint" (12:32) — in her new relationship with the Beloved Disciple (19:25-27).

In the later confrontation with the Jews in the temple, confusion again reigns in regard to Jesus' impending Passion. His disciples finally understand His teaching, however, but again, only after His resurrection (2:19-22).

Dynamic Differences

Jesus transformed the water at the Cana wedding. What is something you have really enjoyed transforming during the last year?

_____

_____

_____

_____

_____

_____

002

Discovery and Discussion

John 2, New International Version

Please read the description of the wedding reception in verses 1-11.

Read verse 5 again and note Mary's response. What do you think gave her the ability to express faith in Him when He had never performed a miracle before?

_____

_____

How would you have felt to have been this young couple and have the name of Jesus in your guest book?

_____

_____

If you had been the groom, what would have been your response to their statement in **verse 10**?

_____

_____

Can you think of three or four reasons why Jesus might have chosen to begin His ministry with this particular miracle? _____

_____

(Perhaps it is important to note here that when this married couple faced a problem, Jesus had the answer!)

What is your first reaction when you face a problem:

    __ work harder   __ complain

    __ cry   __ praise the Lord

    __ ask someone for help   __ give up

    __ pray   __ _____

How do you feel about your answer? _____

_____

An unusual event is described in **verses 13-16**. Please read it carefully.

What emotions do you sense are implied in **verse 15 and 16**?

_____

_____

_____

If you had been sitting at one of the money tables, what would you have done right after this happened?

_____

_____

Where might you have gone?

_____

It is the work of Jesus to drive out of our lives all of those things that should not be there. Think for a moment of your own personal habits and ask Him whether there are any from which He would like to cleanse you right now.

THE TEMPLE IN JESUS' DAY

Although He has just begun His ministry, already there is an ominous prediction in **verse 19**. What did Jesus mean?

_____

_____

_____

In **verse 22** we learn what happened to the disciples when the predictions Jesus made actually happened. Does that suggest why it is helpful to understand prophecy today? _____ (You might ask your group leader if you would like to have some reading material on fulfilled prophecy.)

Please read carefully verse 25.

What does this verse mean to you? Does it give you cause for alarm or for encouragement? Please explain.

_____

_____

_____

13When it was almost time for the Jewish Passover, Jesus went up to Jerusalem. 14In the temple courts he found men selling cattle, sheep and doves, and others sitting at tables exchanging money. 15So he made a whip out of cords, and drove all from the temple area, both sheep and cattle; he scattered the coins of the money changers and overturned their tables. 16To those who sold doves he said, "Get these out of here! How dare you turn my Father's house into a market!"

17His disciples remembered that it is written: "Zeal for your house will consume me."

18Then the Jews demanded of him, "What miraculous sign can you show us to prove your authority to do all this?"

19Jesus answered them, "Destroy this temple, and I will raise it again in three days."

20The Jews replied, "It has taken forty-six years to build this temple, and you are going to raise it in three days?" 21But the temple he had spoken of was his body. 22After he was raised from the dead, his disciples recalled what he had said. Then they believed the Scripture and the words that Jesus had spoken.

Digging Deeper

Describe events that established the Jewish celebration of "Passover." Exodus 12.

_____

_____

_____

_____

In what way can Jesus be our Passover today? 1 Corinthians 5:7.

_____

_____

The earthly temple was originally, in the time of the Exodus, a moving tent (tabernacle). How can the services of the ancient tabernacle and its priests, and Jesus' actions in the temple of His day help us understand Jesus' ministry in heaven for us now? Read especially Hebrews 9.

_____

_____

_____

What is the temple of the Holy Spirit on earth today? 1 Corinthians 6:19 and 20. How do you feel about this?

_____

_____

Disseminating Delight

In what ways can we share the delight of Jesus' transforming power with a friend today? _____

_____

LITHO U.S.A. CP40659

Bibliography

Arn, Win, et al. *Who Cares About Love?* Pasadena, Calif.: Church Growth Press, 1986.

Bainton, Roland. *Christendom.* New York: Harper and Row, 1964.

Barker, Steve, et al. *Small Group Leader's Handbook.* Downers Grove, Ill.: InterVarsity Press, 1982.

Bell, Skip. *Together in Christ.* Grants Pass, Oreg.

Davies, J. G. *The Early Christian Church.* Garden City, N.Y.: Double Day and Company, 1965.

Dillenberger, John, and Claude Welch. *Protestant Christianity.* New York: Charles Scribner and Sons, 1954.

Dudley, Roger L., and Des Cummings, Jr. *Adventures in Church Growth.* Hagerstown, Md.: Review and Herald Pub. Assn., 1983.

Evans, Larry R. *From Cell to Celebration.* Clackamas, Oreg.: Neighborhood Home Bible Study, 1989.

Evans, Louis H., Jr. *Covenant to Care.* Wheaton, Ill.: Victor Books, 1982.

Finley, Mark. *Decisions.* Takoma Park, Md.: General Conference of Seventh-day Adventists, 1984.

Gentz, William H. *The Dictionary of Bible and Religion.* Nashville, Tenn.: Abingdon Press, 1986.

Goodloe, Robert W.; Hutchinson, Paul; and Luccock, Halford E. *The Story of Methodism.* Nashville, Tenn.: Abingdon Press, 1926.

Hestenes, Roberta. *Using the Bible in Groups.* Philadelphia, Pa.: Westminster Press, 1983.

How to Lead Small Group Bible Studies. Colorado Springs, Colo.: NavPress, 1982.

Peace, Richard. *Small Group Evangelism.* Downers Grove, Ill.: InterVarsity Press, 1985.

Schaff, Philip. *History of the Christian Church,* vols. 1 and 2. Grand Rapids, Mich.: Eerdmans Pub. Co., 1959.

Spalding, Arthur W. *Origin and History of Seventh-day Adventists,* vol. 1. Washington, D.C.: Review and Herald Pub. Assn., 1961.

Unger, Merrill F. *Unger's Bible Dictionary.* Chicago, Ill.: Moody Press, 1966.

White, Ellen G. *Counsels to Parents and Teachers.* Mountain View, Calif.: Pacific Press Pub. Assn., 1913.

_____. *Early Writings.* Washington, D.C.: Review and Herald Pub. Assn., 1882.

_____. *Evangelism.* Washington, D.C.: Review and Herald Pub. Assn., 1946.

_____. *Gospel Workers.* Washington, D.C.: Review and Herald Pub. Assn., 1948.

_____. *Testimonies for the Church,* vols. 8, 9. Mountain View, Calif.: Pacific Press Pub. Assn., 1948.

_____. *The Great Controversy.* Mountain View, Calif.: Pacific Press Pub. Assn., 1911.

_____. *The Ministry of Healing.* Mountain View, Calif.: Pacific Press Pub. Assn., 1942.

_____. *This Day With God.* Washington, D.C.: Review and Herald Pub. Assn., 1979.

_____. *Welfare Ministry.* Washington, D.C.: Review and Herald Pub. Assn., 1952.

Williams, Garrie F. *Trinity Power Circle.* Clackamas, Oreg.: Neighborhood Home Bible Study, 1989.

Wollen, Albert J. *Miracles Happen in Group Bible Study.* Glendale, Calif.: Regal Books, G. L. Publications, 1976.